ECHOES OF THE GOLDEN

Kalu Onwuka

𝕲𝕻

Granada Publishers

Los Angeles, California

Echoes of the Golden

Copyright ©2014 by Kalu Onwuka

Published in Los Angeles, California by Granada Publishers. Granada Publishers is wholly owned by Granada Publishing Company, Los Angeles, California.

Granada Publishing titles may be purchased in bulk for educational, fundraising or sales promotional use. For more information please e-mail **sales@granadapublishing.com**

Library of Congress Cataloging-in-Publications Data

Echoes of the Golden/ Kalu Onwuka

LCCN: 2014918590

ISBN: 978-0-9900203-8-7

ISBN: 099002038X

Printed in the United States

DEDICATION

I will like to dedicate this book, *Echoes of the Golden* which is the part of *Ruminations on the Golden Strand* series, to all those who truly share the gifts of light and love everywhere in the world either in formal or informal settings. Yours is not an easy job for truth is very hard to tell and often falls on deaf ears in a world where the sweet and easy has become the norm. The world may or may not acclaim you but Heaven's promise is never to forget or forsake such as you that labor to keep the gate against the onslaught of darkness.

ACKNOWLEDGMENTS

As always, I will first like to acknowledge Christ Jesus as the Lord of my life. He is my muse and I write through his light. Also, I will like to acknowledge that it is not possible to see through an undertaking such as *Ruminations of the Golden Strand* series without the loyal support of family, friends and well-wishers. You have all been there from the beginning on through to the publication process. I will like to acknowledge all your assistance for you continue to give me cause to hope for the best in mankind. It is such goodness that you show that will help transform the world from what is today to the better that it can be in the future.

CONTENTS

CONTENTS

INTRODUCTION

This book titled *Echoes of the Golden* consists of selected works from the author's well-received *Ruminations from the Golden Strand* series. The series which include *Nuggets of Resurrection, Pulses of the Divine Heart, Etching for the Heart,* and *No Hurry to Horeb* encapsulate experiences gleaned during my faith walk and spiritual transformation in following after the teaching of Christ Jesus. There are also numerous insights and observations drawn from real life's experiences that help frame the underlying message in a way that every reader will find to be very enriching.

The book begins by exploring mankind's spiritual estrangement from God and the need for each man to reconnect to his divine roots before his time on earth expires. It reminds mankind, in case some have forgotten, that God watches from above in a search for those worthy to be exalted in spirit to join his company for eternity.

Mankind can never know true fulfillment or have peace within until he makes that spiritual connection with God. This volume explores the steps that mankind can take through faith in the light of Christ Jesus so that he can begin the journey to be reconnected with the divine. It is in this light that a great effort has been made to explore this remarkable journey which in effect transforms mankind's spirit into that of the divine if followed to completion. The seeker that has been fully transformed in spirit has escaped from the misguided past mired in worldliness into a pristine future full of hope in the immunity of Godliness. It is in light of this transformation that the virtue of sacrificial love which purifies baseman into the ever-living that twinkles in hope from within through Christ Jesus is explored.

Often times, truth is bitter to the taste initially but inevitably turns sweet in the due season. The word of God truth often discomforts and makes mankind squirm but amazingly it brings healing with it. The heart that receives words of Truth in good faith has invited divine light to search and shine into its dark recesses. Truth makes all bare in true light so that one can do a valid audit of his life and make the necessary corrections. The 'make over' of the believer's life starts from within and works itself without over time. When the inner man is suitably rehabilitated the outer man cannot help but follow along for the outer is a reflection of the inner.

The act of mercy as an immensely useful and productive investment in the spiritual toolbox of the follower after Christ is covered in this volume. Mercy works in a paradoxical way, for it abounds when expended and shrinks when withheld. The realm of mercy is a place very close to the heart of God. It is the preserve of the worthy in Christ and the spiritual realm of the sons of light whose wishes the heavenly Father delights in granting.

The fate and fortune of humanity rests with the young. In today's world many parents have become distracted by love of worldly materials and have put their offspring at great risk of spiritual death thereby. The distracted parent will fail to shield the child from the enemy of light and prince of darkness bent on destroying mankind's offspring. The enemy of the light of Christ seeks to corrupt the fruit of the tree. He seeks to corrupt the children so that humanity's collective soul is bound with him in the bowels of the earthen. The earthen is miry clay that traps all that is bound therein in consuming convulsions of envy and strife where nothing fulfilling is ever borne.

A great point is made within these pages that more than necessary or inordinate focus on the things of the world is a great trap for many who profess a desire to seek after God. The hunger for the material is a great inhibitor of man's faith. The love of the things of the world results in the neglect and rejection of the ways of God. The way of God and that of the world are opposed to each other. There is no compromise between the two. The heavenly Father is a faithful God but a jealous one. He leaves man with the choice to follow which way his heart desires. It is this choice determined solely by the desires of each man that prescribes the spiritual path that he will take.

The book makes an interesting correlation between the

digital and spiritual world where the sons of light can be viewed as connected to the universal mind of God through Christ. In that light, each son is so connected more or less like a personal computer to a supercomputer God along with a host of other personal computers. The Holy Spirit is the medium that affords the electrical power while the Holy Ghost affords the information within this pseudo-digital world. Each son of God is given a new name which actually works as the password into the network. All knowledge and needed help on how to do all things can be accessed through this network. This is the universal web of life links all that have been received into the divine household and the living church of Christ where the spirits of the just men being perfected in mercy congregate.

The point is also made that there is the perfecting impetus still pulses even within the matured in spirit that has come into the Father through Christ. The fact that the faithful has come to full spiritual transformation does not mean that he has become perfect. No one is ever perfect save God. Infinity may appear to be tantalizingly close but it will ever remain out of reach. It beckons ahead and the faithful can come close enough to it through God's perfecting process. The perfecting agent is the Holy Ghost that speaks to the purified heart so that he may know all that he needs to know and thereby be guided in divine light.

It is also shown within this volume how each son of light has found reconciliation with God to be subsequently at peace within and with all things in creation. Such hear the inaudible whispers that come from all that surround mankind. The ear of the spirit of such pick up much of what everything around is communicating. The sons in effect become wireless receivers that walk about in a sea of information that most men are not aware of. It is by being tuned to the Divine in this wise that man can be sure of where he is going in life and to live that purposed life that produces much good fruits to God's delight.

The fact that the source of the darkness of the world has to be brought under subjugation by the light of Christ under the will of God through his sons acting individually and collectively on earth is presented as a divine imperative. Only then can the groundswell in re-creating the earth in heavenly order happen and lead to the great dawn of humanity. The earth and mankind is God's prized creation but the prince of the darkness of the world has made a mockery of it with his seductive but false ways. He has led humanity down the path of futility, dissatisfaction, emptiness, diseases, simmering conflicts, wars and hopelessness. But his time is fast running out as there is a growing disenchantment with the world's way.

A common mistake that professed seekers after Christ often make is fully examined. One cannot look backwards and forwards at the same time as he follows after Christ Jesus. He will become stagnated in faith and not be able to meet up with Christ if he does so. The enemy of light beguiles the unwary into double-mindedness or uncertainty of faith. First the believer must make the disconnection from the old ways so that he may meet up with Christ. It is only after the seeker has become transformed in spirit and met up with Christ that he can go back to try to change the old for better as love urges him in accordance with God's will.

The faithful meets up with Christ in the future and not in the past. All the great things that he will accomplish in Christ will take place in his future for the past holds no stake for him. He must forget all the injustice that has been done to him in the past. He must leave vengeance and judgment to the God of justice whose timing is always perfect. The tribulations of the past serve to prepare and strengthen the seeker after Christ in spirit. Every true seeker must keep his eyes on the prize ahead for he that returns to the places of the past can neither meet nor keep up with Christ. Every seeker must be in the instant so as to remain ready at all times to answer God's call.

The book also offers encouragement by emphasizing that no one begins his walk with God full of faith. It takes some time to learn to fly on the wings of faith. It takes some time to master how to walk in the fullness of the riches of God through Christ. It takes some time to un-wrap the burial bandages of the old self for the new to step out in fullness of the spirit matured in Christ. He that is fully matured in Christ has become a son of covenant for all ages. Nothing in Heaven above or earth below can separate him from the love of God. He has obtained an irreversible gift where the heavenly Father has made a cleft for him to become grafted to the Divine.

This volume also deals with such things that grieve God's heart such as spiritual hypocrisy among others. The Holy Scriptures implore mankind to be careful not to mock God. But a more insidious but by no means less spiteful way by which man mocks God is through spiritual hypocrisy. Most know and talk about what God requires of man but sadly are not able to live as they profess. Religion abounds in many shapes, forms and congregations but a spiritual famine besets humanity. Evil and wickedness reign in the hearts of mankind. Mankind must watch out for spiritual hypocrisy as it opens the door of divine judgment.

The people of God perish not for lack of good effort but mostly for lack of knowledge. The faithful must seek to know and to live according to knowledge and wisdom. He that abounds in knowledge and wisdom will be protected from the evil in the world to abound in goodness and mercy. This book is not a substitute for the Holy Bible but only serves to amplify the eternal truths contained therein. As the reader ruminates through this volume, I hope that the truth laid bare within the pages will help enlighten minds and reshape hearts into vessels that honor Truth and love so that humanity can become better.

Kalu Onwuka

The way to the source of life points upwards

Tis not found by bravado, might or strength

But by the sincere, humble and lowly in spirit

In the light of truth, charity, peace and love

Chapter 1

FINDING THE WAY HOME

The truly faithful in Christ find much nourishment in the unleavened bread of God's truth. Often times bitter to the taste initially, Truth inevitably turns sweet after it is received in good faith. The words of truth may discomfort and make the hearer squirm but it embodies the spirit of healing. Good medicine is often bitter but it makes the sick better. The word of truth when wholly embraced will purify the soul and nourish the spirit within. The heart that receives Truth well has invited divine light to search and shine into its dark recesses. Truth makes all things bare so that one can do a valid audit of his life and make necessary corrections. The 'make over' of the believer's life starts from within and works itself without over time. When the inner man is suitably rehabilitated the outer cannot help but follow suit for the latter is a reflection of the former.

God's truth welcomed into the heart and amply accommodated helps to transform the spirit within in the likeness of the Divine. The spirit that is fully transformed has grown to full maturity in Christ and is able to soar to the divine realm. He that is fully transformed in this light will become a custodian of the sacred. He will be given the Holy Ghost which affords man the means to partake in conversations in heavenly places. He that has been bestowed with such a spirit is a vessel chosen for mighty works that will bring glory and praise to God. Every chosen vessel will be well attended by Providence for his prayers and petitions will be answered as the need arises.

To be of glorious service in this wise, the mind has to be set on things that will be deemed worthy, lovely and of a good report before God. Such things that are well commended in Heaven turn out to be the amazing on earth. The faithful in Christ has to be well informed and know to ask for such as he makes his petitions to God. The spirit may be free to soar to the heavenly realm but if the mind is filled with worldly or earthy thoughts then petitions and prayers will come to naught. The faithful are called to translate the heavenly on earth and not the other way around. The professed seeker after Christ whose mind is filled with the worldly will profit nothing in the kingdom of God. The spirit has to be pure and the mind focused on the heavenly to be deemed worthy of use for the amazing. He that is matured in Christ that seeks with a pure heart and focused mind can indeed do all things through Christ.

It takes strong faith and great vision to master the way of

Christ for it is the heavenly totally contrary to the earthly. It is on the heaven-bound way that all things become known and the shadowy becomes exposed. It is there in the realm of greater illumination that the faithful seeker meets up with Christ Jesus to become christened in light as a son of Heaven. But it takes many years of devotion to come into greater enlightenment. He that seeks must be willing to shed the cloudy teachings under which he has labored during his years of spiritual growth so that he can rendezvous with Christ. He must put away the childish so that he can become a man of God. To come into greater enlightenment is to no longer see darkly through a mirror but to see in reality. It is the difference between seeing a country in a travelogue and being there in person. Every true seeker must put away the rudimentary and misguided teachings of the past. The rudimentary embodies the burial bandages that bind the resurrected 'Lazarus'. Such must be peeled away so that the man of God can come forth. It is the dirt of false gold that must be washed away so that the true gold concealed within can shine forth.

Every vessel chosen to do the good works of Christ must have compassion for the spiritually blind. Many who profess to follow in the way of Christ are still spiritually immature. They know in part but not fully. Such are of the concision and not of the circumcision. Sadly many that know in part are not aware of it because they trudge along under rudimentary teachings and misguided assumptions that reflect long held traditions that are of little or no spiritual value at all. Their vision is clouded and limited at best to the tip of the nose and not to the horizon as should be. Such that are being led in their judgments by the opinions of men and the traditions of the past forget that God is always opening up new veins of the Divine for the faithful to mine. He is always opening new doors and revealing new vistas as he patiently brings man along on the way of righteousness. The heavenly Father uses time to filter and purify man's soul as he patiently prepares him in the way of divinity. The traditions of the past constitute a veil that must be lifted so that man can clearly see. It is a membrane that must be punctured so that the new man of Christ can be 'born'. Christ does not come to regurgitate the old. He distills the old to extract the relevant and dispense with the irrelevant. The latter is mostly fluffy and hypocritical chaff. This is the leaven of the Pharisee that the sons of light are constantly bemoaning.

He that has come into greater enlightenment to meet up with Christ has come into a chosen and special place. He will be falsely accused and wrongly judged not so much for breaking new grounds but rather for discarding the tools of the past. The tools of the past are worn out and ill-suited to break the new grounds that God has preserved for the chosen. The tools of the past are flesh-centric whereas the tools of the new are spirit-centric. It helps to think of it as the difference between the industrial age of yesteryears and the information age of today. It requires information technology know-how to be able to navigate today's digital world. Only those with the requisite knowledge can benefit from its myriad utilities and applications. The fully matured in Christ are enmeshed in an unfathomable mine of divine wisdom where God urges them to search deeper and patiently informs their mind in a never ending perfecting process.

The heavenly way availed through Christ is like new wine that must be contained in new vessels. The latter are the fully matured in Christ and christened in light to be sons of God. He that has been reborn in divine light must have compassion for the ignorance of many. He must constantly ask God for forgiveness on behalf of such for the new vessels are often misunderstood. Each new vessel knows that he has been anointed for a special mission and that so much has been entrusted into his care by God. He must use the same measure and weights for everyone. He must be a model of the golden rule that demands that each treat the other as they would like to be treated. There must be no in-equity found in him. He must espouse that form of justice that judges the inner man and not the outer. He must be the righteous judge before God and man whose high calling is to expose spiritual wickedness on earth. He must speak for the poor, the powerless and those without voice. The matured in light has been called to help pull out roots of evil borne from the rejection of truth from men's hearts and to help mankind cast off the fake mask used to make accommodation for the untrue.

He that has fully matured in light to meet up with Christ has come into the knowledge of all wisdom. He must live charitably and use the gifts entrusted to him for the welfare of humanity. He must be the light of God to his blind fellows. He is that sinner once forgiven that has become justified before God through Christ. And so he is given to travel through life in the company of an unseen host as a member of the divine household. All who have met up with Christ are spiritual 'giants' who walk under the cloak of divinity among men to carry out the will of God in their assigned 'lots' on earth. It is the worthiest of callings where the inner man is not bound by the earthen but can bear all things. He that can overcome the world in spirit has learnt to defy and rise above 'gravity'. He can rise from the grave in the new for he has buried his old self together with the cares and worries of the world with Christ. He that defies gravity is irrepressible in spirit and can rise to the heavenly realm. He that is laden with the care of the earthy material can never overcome the world. He will never learn how to rise above the world and master how to soar in spirit to the heavenly realm.

The gift of flight is man's ultimate dream come true. It is the completion of the journey that he begun from the salty sea through the earthly plane to end hopefully in his original home in the heavens. It is the journey that ends in triumphant escape to the better that all the great herds in creation are searching to find. They fail to find the way because it is found on the road less travelled. It is found by the sojourner on earth led along by the Spirit of the heavenly Father. The search for the way of escape is mimicked in the migration of countless creatures that travel in herds. The rendezvous with the Divine is not realized in a herd or group for each must bear his own cross after Christ. All creatures that have life coursing through them have a deep longing to return home to the source of creation. But only a few will find the way back through the tunnel of light into the womb of dawn.

The faithless that is unpurified in spirit is a creature of the flesh. Creatures with unpurified souls engage in a fruitless and ceaseless search that can never be satisfied because they search for an earthly home. They can only search on earth because their souls are weighty and encrusted with the worldly. But that which they search for can only be found in the heavenly realm above. The spirit is the wind that lifts the soul upwards. The unpurified soul lacks the spirit to lift upwards but the purified soul is buoyant and takes flight easily. The way home to the source of all creation points upwards and is found in the exalted heights where the free spirits soar. It is not found by bravado, might or power. The way is found through humility, sincerity, charity and peace. The way up is found through the lowly. He that soars in light is often deemed to be of a low degree by the world but such has been exalted by God to join him in divine company. The call to come home to God is the way for man to know self so as to be true to all. It is the call that echoes down through time and for all ages. Man's true home lies in his heavenly future and not through his earthly past. The beast of unpurified soul looks for a home in his earthly past but the purified soul seeks a new home in his heavenly future.

The heavenly home is a continuing city that will never pass away. That is where the search ends and satisfaction is found. He that persists in searching for a home through his earthly past is nothing but a beast unpurified of soul that will remain a victim and never know victory. He will exhaust his limited time on earth in an endless and fruitless search that will leave him wondering at the end what the quest has been all about. He that has learned to rise above the world and mastered how to soar to the heavenly heights has received the key of knowledge. He will have a divine perspective for he too can be the eye that sees and knows all. He must set about taking care of the heavenly father's business on earth. It is the mission that he has been prepared and empowered to carry out. And so, there is no time for such to waste but to carry on with it. He must dissociate from all things that negate and subtract from the mission of Christ. He must be willing to carry on alone if need be but he will never be alone for he is ever in the company of an innumerable divine host. He must dwell therein secure in light, peace, and love where nothing can touch him but glory patiently waits.

- ✓ The word of Truth may discomfort and make man squirm but it embodies the spirit of healing.
- ✓ The fully matured in Christ has been prepared to do mighty works that bring praise and glory to God.
- ✓ The mind that is set on the lovely that is of good report will soar in spirit to the heavenly heights.
- ✓ Rudimentary and misguided teachings of the past must be peeled away for the reborn to come forth.
- ✓ Many who profess to follow in light after Christ are spiritual children who know in part but not in full.
- ✓ The tools of the past are worn out and ill-suited to break the new grounds reserved for the reborn.
- ✓ The reborn in spirit must espouse justice that assays the inner man and not the outer.
- ✓ He that has overcome the world has a spirit freed from the burden of earthly cares and worries.
- ✓ The heavenly home is not found by bravado, might or power but in humility, sincerity and peace.
- ✓ The source of creation points upwards and is found in the realm where the free in spirit congregate.
- ✓ The spirit of man can only find fulfillment in the eternal realm for there all searches end.
- ✓ The fully reborn in Christ dwells where nothing can touch the spirit but glory waits with open arms.
- ✓ Rebirth in divine light brings about an illumination that connects man to God's all-knowing wisdom.

Eternity becomes the final destination

When man's footsteps seek after God

Such will come into realm of delights

And join the everlasting song in joy

Chapter 2

STARS OF HEAVEN

The act of mercy is an immensely useful and productive spiritual asset in the portfolio of the follower after Christ. Mercy works in a paradoxical way, for it abounds when tendered and shrinks when withheld. The realm of mercy is a place very close to the Divine heart. It is the preserve of those who have proven worthy in Christ to become known by God. It is the spiritual realm of the sons of God whose wishes the Father delights to grant. To grow into full maturity in light through Christ subjects the faithful to much suffering and hurt at the hands of the worldly. The believer will suffer not only at the hands of unbelieving strangers but also family, friends and acquaintances. The faithful believer is often taken advantage of, put to ridicule, blatantly lied against, wrongfully accused and mostly misjudged.

Such a faithful one is called to endure and persevere through his heartaches and pains. It is the only way for the ego of the flesh to be decreased so that the inner man of the spirit can increase. It is all very hurtful for the seeker but it is in fact necessary because the flesh does not yield easily to the spirit. All the injustices heaped upon the faithful believer add up to the process of crucifixion by which the old self is buried so that the new man of the spirit can be realized. For man to begin to ascend in spirit, he must pass through the figurative eye of the needle. The latter separates the heavenly from the earthly. It takes crucifixion to streamline mind, body and spirit so as to be able to pass through the eye of the needle for ascension to the exalted heights.

The faithful that is able to ascend in spirit has come to the heavenly side of the cross. The benefits found there far outweigh the agony of crucifixion. He that has come to the heavenly side must learn to be merciful to all who wrong and grieve him. It is the only way that he can be able to share and abound in the Hope that he has found for the tender mercies of God will follow him everywhere. The treasure trove of mercy is immense and exhaustless. The tender mercies are promised, received and enjoyed through forgiving love. There is no recrimination or bitterness mixed in with mercy. The sunshine of divine love always shines in mercy with joyful exuberance and cannot wait for the dawn of each morning. It cannot wait for the birds to chirp. It cannot wait for the flower to unfold. The sunshine of love cannot wait to hear the sweet melody of life playing once again. Every son of God is borne in love and is a 'sun' of righteousness. Therefore each son must strive to keep the flame of divine love alive in his heart by forgetting the hurt rendered to him by all for that is the essence of mercy and the good life.

In order to come into the full anointing of God, the faithful believer must do away with the needless things that clutter his life. He must simplify and arrange his priorities in life so that orderliness can be established. Doing so allows for the focus to be put on the things that will prove to be lovely and of a good report. This re-arrangement or pruning of his life allows the faithful believer to find the core of his true self. It is this core that responds readily to Truth. The faithful believer has to go through this pruning alone within a sort of wilderness in life. It is in this season when he is seemingly alone and forsaken by many that he is able to understand the true essence of the Divine. It is in this season that the believer comes to know fully and to begin to see in the clarity of the higher and purer. This is when he will begin to live life fully as Christ reborn and less in conformity with the world for he has entered where the flesh profits nothing but the spirit profits everything.

When the faithful ceases to live in conformity with the world, he will enter into a commencement of true confession. His words will become few and measured. He will only speak the much needed to bear testimony about Truth. It has to be so for his heart has become the wellspring of life out of which flows living water. He has become a man of certainty who will not compromise his faith and so must guard his tongue. Such that has become a fountain of life must strive to remain righteous for God now commands his obedience in all things and at all times.

He that has yielded his will to God has escaped from the domain of shadows into the realm of light where confusion abates and serenity reigns over the soul. God's grace has enabled him to scale the ladder of faith through Christ. He has been lifted into the realm of mercy to become one able to overcome and garner victory over the enemy. Many who strive to come into the realm of mercy fail on account of love for the material things of the world. In loving the world to a fault, they leave little room in themselves to be filled with the requisite measure of the essence of godliness needed to overcome the world. Therefore they remain bound to the world as sons of men and are not able to escape its shackles as sons of God.

The faithful believer that has been lifted in spirit into the realm of mercy is soon revealed to all who are perceptive by the Heavenly Father. He that has buried the flesh of his old self and forsaken the world for love of God through Christ comes to be duly acknowledged in due season. This acknowledgement comes in form of the ability to receive information and knowledge flashed into the mind through the Holy Ghost. He will become tuned in spirit to the inaudible voice of the Holy Ghost that brings affirming and comforting thoughts from the mind of the Father above to his sons below. He that has been lifted into the realm of mercy will know what to pray for and when to pray for it for he has entered the season of the refreshing of the latter rain. Such will cease to labor in his own flesh but be enabled rather by the spirit of God in his endeavors. He will face many temptations and fight many spiritual battles. But to his advantage, he will always have fore knowledge through the Holy Ghost to help prepare him for victory through his troubles.

The faithful one tuned in spirit to the Holy Ghost can battle and defeat the enemy because he will always have informed and insightful knowledge in all situations. Most believers perish at the hands of the enemy for lack of informed knowledge about what is going on around them in life. The Holy Ghost provides that hidden and inside knowledge that most who profess to follow Christ do not have access to. By extension, the believer tuned in spirit to hear the Holy Ghost becomes the bearer of light in a dark world. Such have been prepared and stationed as lighthouses all over the world to guide those given to embrace Truth through the storms of life into safe harbor. Each son is a giant of faith who has been given the Holy Ghost to inform him about things and the Holy Spirit to help him make things happen. The Holy Ghost is the ample brain and the Holy Spirit ample brawn that embody the spiritual giant or Colossus of faith.

Each spiritual giant (as a son of God) has the potential to do all things and can initiate the trend of things on earth.

He is assigned an earthly plot and handed the script of life. The script of life frames the battle of good against evil and light over darkness. The earthly plot is a drama stage that depicts life on which character actors are called to play certain roles in good faith. Their roles have already been ordained by the Heavenly Father. All will be judged on how well they perform their roles for there is an award at the end. Each son is like a director that guides others on how to give laudable performances that will please God on life's grand stage. The Heavenly Father is the executive producer but he has anointed each son to be a director of events on the earthly lot ordained for him. Each son must always have the right script by having his mind focused on the heavenly so that he can turn out a winning production as expected of him. He must direct every stage production so that good defeats evil and light triumphs over darkness as should. To do otherwise is to engage in an unwinnable fight with Omnipotence. To veer off the assigned script is an attempt to upset the apple cart of Heaven.

- ✓ Mercy is a useful and productive spiritual tool in the treasure chest of the matured in light.
- ✓ Love learns to forgive the injustice and injuries suffered at the hands of others.
- ✓ There must be no recrimination so that the promises of love can be duly received and enjoyed.
- ✓ The faithful that puts his life in good order is able to put focus on the things that matter with God.
- ✓ The tongue that speaks in testimony to Truth must be well-guarded and speak only measured words.
- ✓ The faithful that yields to the Divine will escape from darkness to have serenity reign over the soul.
- ✓ Each son is acknowledged and revealed by God to all who are perceptive in spirit in due season.
- ✓ Victory over the enemy is availed by informed and insightful knowledge about the important in life.
- ✓ God assigns a plot to be cultivated into a garden of fruitful trees to every faithful believer.

The long running drama of life below

Is a motion picture for those above

Tis apples of gold turned in due time

'to pictures of silver witnessed by all

Chapter 3

THE WALK OF FAME

The star lit night is the silver screen and canvas that reflects the earthly handiworks of the sons of God in twinkling majesty. Each son is a golden award director whose masterful work is held up in immortal display for mere mortals to gaze at. The glory of God shed on his sons leave mere mortals star-struck for their works do indeed shine brilliantly before mankind. Everyone that is willing to embrace Truth is cast for a role in the grand performance of life. There are different roles and parts to play in life's drama but it is divinely assigned through pre-destination. All whose eyes have been opened to understand this must perform their roles with brilliant honor. The role performed with brilliant honor is the life lived in faith and Truth in the service of goodness to humanity. The audience is the heavenly host that watches, judges and records all the earthly performances of mankind.

The faithful who have passed judgment before God are deemed worthy to be exalted to the starry heights. Such are deemed worthy to join the troupe of celestial stars who perform in endless majesty on the ultra-grand stage of the night sky. Every faithful one who has been well received by God has been planted to shine in light as a star of heaven. Each star must have some satellite planets that revolve around them for every son must bear offspring in the way of light. The satellite planets are those believers who have embraced Truth to come into knowledge of the Divine through the sons. The satellites are the wise virgins who fill their lamps with oil and wait patiently for the bridegroom in order to become 'married' to him.

The believers 'married' to the sons through faith are like plants in the garden given to be pollinated by the tree of righteousness in their midst. The tree of righteousness is that which stands when other trees are long gone. Some trees have been cut down and used for firewood. Others were struck by lightning and split apart. Some could not survive the strong winds and were blown down. Some could not survive the season of drought because they craved for much. Others were washed away in the season of the floods. Yet others could not survive the scourge of marauding and myriad infestations. The tree of righteousness is the lone tree that stands through all that felled others. It withstands the fire that burns the grass that clutters the land. The grass is that which seeks and lives for the praise of men. But the tree of righteousness is he that bears testimony to the power and faithfulness of God as he watches over the beloved flock. Each son of God is a tree of righteousness called to pollinate the plants that God has placed in his earthly lot for such will grow to full maturity and produce good fruits in their appointed seasons. Such is the reasonable service and laudable performance that translates the earthly into the heavenly as well as transform the mortal into immortality.

The book of life is the index of credits that lists the names of those who have performed their roles on earth with honor to Heaven's acclaim. Each son is a guiding light that illuminates the way so that the spiritually blind may find the way back to the Heavenly Father. Such is a member of the living church that is the congregation of Christ. He lives to bring men closer to the knowledge of God by translating the heavenly ways on earth. The anointing of Christ is bestowed on the sons so that they can untie the knots of spiritual bondage, lift the veil of spiritual blindness, obtain forgiveness for the sinful and resuscitate the moribund among mankind. It is the same anointing yesterday, today and forever given to make the dead in spirit to live again in the light of Truth in love. It is the same Truth shared and well taken to heart that make sons of God out of mortal men. It is the same redeeming light that shines brilliantly into the dark recesses of hearts to chase away the fears and torments of darkness forever.

Each son of heaven belongs to the vanguard of greater enlightenment divinely chosen to bring a deeper and better understanding of the heavenly ways to blind humanity. Each is an illuminator that helps to highlight and process the meat of spiritual Truth for clearer and better understanding. Each son is a man of strong faith and courage who can be entrusted with due new knowledge by the Father. By them do men come into the knowledge of new things that flow from the heavenly throne. They are such that speak with certain knowledge for they have known God's unfailing faithfulness. The knowledge that they have is conveyed by the Holy Ghost and the assurance that they possess is affirmed by the Holy Spirit. He that has both the Holy Ghost and the Holy Spirit is an oracle of the Divine that speaks with truthful courage. The oracle is the voice of divine reasoning that seeks to guide mankind back on to the path of righteousness. The oracle does not use his gift for personal gain but to tend the sheep of God's flock. The oracle speaks to specific situations and clamors not for the artificial light of the world stage but lives in hope for a starring role in the immortalized silver screen up above.

Each son is connected with the Heavenly Father and with the other sons in a web pulsing with life and knowledge. What one son knows the others can know and what one has the others can have too. It is a spiritual commonwealth in which the sons are connected in love. They do not seek for an audience to show what they know for they seek not the praise of men. Rather each son labors to use what he has been entrusted with to bring others into the marvelous light of God through Christ. Such is not overwhelmed by the flood of information that abounds in today's world. He is shielded from the surreptitious and wasteful but guided to that which is needful. He is anchored on solid rock and therefore the overwhelming floods of the present cannot overtake him. He knows the right choices to make, the right answers to give and the right path to walk in life. He is one that always strives to appropriate and use what he has been given to serve God's divine purposes on earth.

Each son must always give a wonderful performance in order to please the eager eyes of the Heavenly Father who watches from his throne above. In order to do so, he must always keep the unclean spirit at bay. The latter is the viral and corrupting impulses that seek to pull him back into that past which he has escaped from. It aims to lead him back with seductive and gentle persistence into the slippery domain of shadows where darkness is not far removed. It seeks to beguile him into life's basement where the decrepit soul makes his home. Each son must be on guard for the unequal yoking that infringes upon his 'life' in God. He must let the dead bury the dead. He has been chosen and kept apart by God. In order to remain so, he will displease many in the short term but in the long term all will thank God for him.

The unclean spirit is a devourer and feasts in the hearts of those who profess Christ but have not partaken worthily of grace. Such heard the message but did not heed faithfully

They picked and chose what to obey or not obey. They performed their undertakings always with an eye for the praise of men and personal gain. The unclean spirit is the spirit of instability and contending opposites that steadily tears apart the soul of its host. Such a host may appear to be okay one day but is deeply troubled the next. It can be likened to a bipolar existence where the host has built his house on shifting sand instead of the solid rock of God through Christ. The unclean spirit aims to chip away at the foundation of faith. It is much like a virus that strikes stealthily to misdirect and confuse the infirm in spirit. Truth is the firewall that protects from the intrusion of the unclean destabilizing spirit. Truth affords passage through the valley of the shadow of death so that the enemy may chase but never catch up to those sanctified by it. If and when the enemy catches up with any sanctified in Truth such will be powerless to do him harm for he has become immune to evil. All who are immune to evil are the overcomers that can indeed do the marvelous in life by faith through Christ. Such are the new vessels and their content the divine new wine.

- ✓ Divine glory shed on mankind make for works that shine brilliantly to leave mortals star struck.
- ✓ Each son is a tree of righteousness divinely planted to pollinate those that are planted in his lot.
- ✓ The book of life is the index of credits that lists the names that have performed honorably on earth.
- ✓ The reborn have been chosen to bring a deeper and better understanding of the heavenly way.
- ✓ The believer in communion with the Divine makes right choices and walks on the right path in life.
- ✓ Worldliness constitutes the viral and corrupting that seek to pull the believer back into an ugly past.
- ✓ The unclean spirit feasts in the hearts of those who profess Christ but do not partake worthily of grace.
- ✓ Truth affords divine immunity to protect and give safe passage through the dark seasons of life.
- ✓ Truth is the firewall that protects from the unclean which makes the spirit within infirm.
- ✓ All who have divine immunity through Christ are given to do the marvelous in life.

To love the Truth and obey in light

Connects to the source of wisdom

And 'to creation's governing order

So that heart's desires can be had

Chapter 4

THE SWEET SPOT

There is a certain and definite order that governs all things in creation. That order was first set in place by God when he created the heavens, earth and everything contained therein. At the present time, it may all appear chaotic and confusing to the uninformed and spiritually blind but that is far from the case. God did not set about to create confusion and chaos as a final outcome. He is never taken by surprise either for he knows all the way from the beginning through to the end of all things. It should then be clearly understood that regardless of how things seem now, the underlying order set down from the beginning by God will prevail at the end when it matters the most. It will become evident to all then that God has always known what he is doing and remains fully in control even though it might not have been obvious to the faithless.

At the fulfillment of the time appointed for this age, all things that are left in creation will come into knowledge of their true place in the divine order. All who have passed judgment in God's eyes will be found standing when that time comes. They will be the ones deemed worthy of spiritual communion and eternal fellowship with the heavenly father. Such are the faithful in the way after Christ worthy to be transformed into his spiritual likeness. Such will continue in glorious fellowship with God as well as others that are righteous before him.

The righteous before him are chosen to be adopted into the divine family by the heavenly Father. They are chosen on account of a life of faithful obedience to the words of Truth and devotion in the way of Christ. Such are fused with the divine ethos because they have yielded to God's will as life's sovereign guide. They persevere to serve the divine will so that everyone that they encounter on earth may be nudged a little towards the Creator. In many ways, their lives on earth have been much like puffs of winds that uplift the willing towards the heavenly Father. Not everyone is receptive to Truth and willing to accept God's offer of redemption through Christ. The faithless that rejects Truth and the light of Christ is precluded from knowledge of the Father and joining the divine household. There is no other recourse for the precluded than for his moribund spirit to return to the base material of the earth. On the other hand the believer that is adopted into the divine family has become bound with God eternally. Such is man's lot when he has found salvation and settled into the place destined for him from the foundation of time.

The heavenly Father always does as he says and will never

do anything without letting his faithful servants know. One of the marvelous things about God is that he hates surprises and will always give advance warnings of his intentions. He will always signal his intentions to those who trust him for guidance. He hates to see anything and anyone in creation suffer needlessly if it can be helped. Sadly it is man that has left the place divinely appointed for him and gone his own way. Yet it is God's desire that those who have gone astray come to be duly reconciled with him. But he also knows that most love the world too much to make the commitment to seek that reconciliation.

But in his forgiving and loving nature, God is willing to suffer indignity in the hope that no true seeker after light is left without hope or stranded in the way. The spirit of the world is noisome so that confusion often reigns and drowns out his voice that pleads with humanity to change course. As one comes to believe in the teachings of Christ Jesus to let the words of Truth guide him in life, the noise of the world will begin to fade for him. He will come to be spiritually untangled from the clutches of the world and to enter into peace availed through Christ. It is in this state of peace that the seeker after Christ begins to be tuned in spirit to the Divine and to see God's handiwork in creation.

The believer begins to hear and see the handiworks of God clearly when he has become alive in the spirit of new life through Christ. It is in this place of spiritual communion that the true servants of God dwell. Since God will never do anything without letting the faithful know, he uses those tuned to him in spirit as his mouthpiece to speak to those that are not. He communicates his intentions to those who can understand him more clearly and uses them to speak to those who understand little about him or not at all. These oracles of God speak from a place veiled to most men but made known to only a few. They speak about things concealed to the earthbound in spirit. The message is often about the sad trend of things on earth and the impending doom for mankind due to his ungodly ways. Yet it always reminds about the gift of Christ as the way of escape from that doom into safe refuge with God.

It only requires the love of truth and belief in the teachings of Christ Jesus for mankind to find that escape and refuge with the heavenly Father. The faithful believer who is committed enough to embrace Truth wholly will be led in spirit through the straight and narrow that is the way of Christ. It is a 'worm hole' that leads away from a world of darkness into a world of light. It is the worm-hole that Jacob the earth-man of dust crawled through to come out transformed as Israel the god-man of glory. It leads from the world of mere mortals into the place of god-men beyond. It is made available to the faithful that seek after God in humility and sincerity for no one can find the way by the works of his own hands. Only those who love the way of Christ unconditionally are chosen and led to find it. The passage through the worm-hole is a gift received by faith through grace with God as the final arbiter.

The place of the god-men beyond where the true servants of God dwell can be likened to the spiritual house top of the earth. It is the top of God's mountain and heaven's table land. The faithful that dwell thereabouts can be likened to communication satellites positioned in that sweet spot between the earth and greater beyond. It is a place inhabited by the spirit that is truly at ease. It is reserved for the noble in spirit who put their trust in God. In putting their trust in God, the faithful do find that place of harmony where there is no perturbing the universal order within creation. They find their places in that order to become vehicles by which divine riches may be availed to mankind. They that dwell on the spiritual rooftops serve to give voice to those things heard with the ear of the spirit in divine light. They never speak unless it is for the common good and benefit of mankind. They will not proselytize their faith nor exploit it for gain. Such are the worthy trustees of divine gifts and faithful custodians of the precious with which they are entrusted.

He that dwells on the spiritual housetop occupies a very special place. His conversation will no longer be about the lowly that pervades today's world but about the heavenly purposed to uplift humanity. He that has joined the conversation in heavenly places is able to prophesy and speak about impending events before they come to pass. In today's world as the time of the fulfillment of all things approaches, he is able to speak about imminent things that are at mankind's doorsteps. He that will be effectively used in this way must get rid of the corruptible from his life. He must not come down from the 'housetop' to get that which he has left behind in the house. He must remain on the housetop so that he can be steeped in heavenly mists and divine dew. He must remain there so that he can be duly informed as well as have insight into the mystifying in life. In order to do so, he must let go of all that are earthbound so that he can stand in the congregation of the mighty for that is his destiny.

He who has grown to dwell on the spiritual housetop must live by the statutes of God. There are things intimately revealed that the faithful must safeguard and hold dear to heart. It is by those things that he will be known and judged. This is the 'Achilles heel' that he must protect so that he is not precluded from standing in the congregation of the mighty. He must observe the statute revealed to him for it is by obedience to such that the spiritual child becomes a man of God. The faithful in light who observes the statute appointed to him will become a statue fashioned in God's own true likeness. He will stand among the congregation of the valiant framed in peace and serenity for all ages to come. He will stand among the Colossus of faith for all who seek knowledge and wisdom to learn from. He will stand with his eye fixed above and will be counted among those who will catch the first rays of the break of mankind's glorious dawn.

The faithful who dwells on the spiritual housetop has

grown to maturity in Christ Jesus. He has chosen to forego all that will keep him earthbound so that he may escape to the exalted place appointed for him among the stars. For such, God's truth is life's guide for therein is woven the golden threads of the eternal that are for the exalted in spirit to truly and fully fathom. The exalted in spirit are able to fully fathom Truth because the wisdom therein is framed in pictures for them to perceive. This exalted place of spiritual escape is the meeting place between the Divine which reaches down from Heaven above and the hopeful spirit which reaches upwards from earth below.

The confluence of the heavenly and earthly is the realm of greater divine illumination. It is in this realm that the harmony of the scriptures can be fully understood and the infallibility of God's truth clearly ascertained. This is the realm where Hope speaks in the still small voice that can be heard and clearly understood within the spirit. It is in this realm that the Truth declared within the words of scripture and the experiences of daily life perfectly agree to confirm the reality of the Divine. The exalted realm is where the glorious concealed by God are known by the noble in spirit deemed of honor before him.

The statutes address the mundane that hold back the upward bound from ascending into the place of glory. The glory belongs to the heavenly Father but he is eager to shed it on those worthy in Christ. There is an appointed season when the seeker must forego certain things in order to come into the knowledge of the Father. It is then that the seeker through Christ separates himself from the world out of own volition so that he can intermeddle with all wisdom. Only in this way can the believer come to the fullness of the knowledge and wisdom of God. It is in this way that he will come into knowledge of God's will and the wisdom of all ages. It is the statute revealed to the faithful in Christ that separates him from all others and makes him to be of effectual use by God. It is the statute that makes him a certain man unto God. It is the statute that certifies that he has placed God above all things in his life. It is by the statute that the faithful is chiseled into a statue that fits into that certain cleft made in the Rock of Ages.

As noted earlier, there is a season of spiritual transition in which the spiritual child becomes a man of God. In that season, all that has been reserved for the faithful in Christ will become his to possess. The vessel must be clean in that season so that there is no corruption and defiling of that which he will be endowed with. There must be no unequal yoking or conforming to those around him who are unworthy of honor before God. This is the season for him to be transformed and he is called to leave those things that are not able to come up to housetop in the house below. He must therefore present himself as a living sacrifice dedicated to be used marvelously to Heaven's glory. He must be willing to step away from the present things that encumber his spirit so that he can be used to secure the future. This is his reasonable service for he has become a son of Heaven by whom many will experience spiritual rebirth and escape imminent judgment. He has also become a depository of the needful that those who have lived in pursuits of the wanted now lack and need. It is in this light and for this purpose that the dweller on the housetop has been chosen to serve as 'savior' for many.

The fulfillment of the events prophesied in earlier times and in the sacred books rest on the sons of Heaven. They are the vehicles or instruments used to make those things come about. They are players in the cosmic drama with significant roles to fulfill. They exercise their power and fulfill their roles through obedience to God's divine will. They constitute the spiritual bulwark that stand against the evil that constantly threatens mankind for their prayers and call to God for help do work wonders. For this reason they are given knowledge of certain events as well as called to share such in the hope that humanity can be spared from trouble ahead or blessed as the case may be.

The faithful entrusted with due knowledge by God labor under a heavy burden. It is a monumental responsibility for them to bear for oftentimes their warnings and counsels are often ignored. Such warnings are met with doubt, ridicule and derision from a dismissive world. The blind that live in a world of darkness can never experience the wonders of enlightenment unless they can be made to 'see'. And so the transformed in Christ, who is a creature of hope, never gives up trying to help the blind see while there is time left and work to be done. He responds to love's urge and spares no effort while there is still one left on the way to be rescued. Only when there is none left to be rescued will his work be done so that he can enter into the rest ordained for him by the heavenly Father.

The knowledge of events glimpsed from behind the veil by the faithful that dwells on the spiritual housetop must be written down faithfully so that there are never forgotten. Such knowledge is like the sprinkling of golden dust from Heaven. It must be safeguarded and put to the benefit of mankind as called for. In such knowledge is gleaned the substance of the everlasting and unchanging with which Heaven is populated. Such knowledge evokes and sustains life itself as well as power that makes old things new. The knowledge and wisdom of God revealed to mankind is solely for the purpose of redemption and rebirth. It assures victory in the battle of light against darkness where the soul of the next generation is at stake. The faithful who seeks after God in the light of Christ may suffer temporary loss in the world but in his house will be laid up much wealth. The wealth laid up therein is not the kind that the world affords but the true wealth that the noble in spirit seek after. These are the needful and enduring things that the predatory spirit cannot touch. These are the good gifts that the heavenly Father assures in love, ensures in light and insures by faith.

- ✓ The underlying order set down from time by God will prevail once again at the end of this age.
- ✓ The faithful walk on earth so that the spirit of every man that they encounter is lifted towards God.
- ✓ The twinkling lights and noise of the world drowns out the voice that pleads with man to change ways.
- ✓ God communicates his intentions to the faithful to uses them to speak to the faithless and blind.
- ✓ The walk after Christ may be considered lowly by the world but it leads from darkness into new life.
- ✓ The sweet spot between the heavenly and earthly is where the order of creation is unperturbed.
- ✓ The faithful that dwells on the spiritual housetop will be steeped in knowledge and wisdom.
- ✓ There is a season to forego certain things in order to meet up with Christ and come into the Father.
- ✓ Duty calls the reborn in light to help others realize spiritual rebirth and escape divine judgment.
- ✓ The sons of God constitute the bulwark that holds evil at bay by their earnest entreaties and prayers.
- ✓ It is only when the faithful finishes the work ordained for him that he enters into faith rest.
- ✓ Wealth appointed for the faithful in light is assured in love, ensured in light and insured in faith.
- ✓ The battle of light against darkness is really for the collective soul of the future generation.

Many often seek and find fool's gold to heart's fill

Blind men who cannot see that the earth is a dump

Constantly being recycled by a non-wasting Minder

Who searches in light of Truth for the redeemable

Chapter 5

PEACE THAT IS PRICELESS

The enemy of Truth, who is the prince of the darkness of the world, is a liar and destroyer. His sole purpose is to lead mankind into a state of spiritual bankruptcy where the creature is honored rather than the Creator. When the creature is honored above his Creator, then the course of goodness is forestalled and the curse of evil installed. The enemy aims to achieve this evil plot by the spiritual strangulation of humanity's collective soul through crave for self-glory. He who loves to hear others sing his praise is a 'Herod' in spirit. Such will slaughter the next generation including his own children for short term gain. But the just that honor the Creator with due praise is given rather to save lives to Heaven's delight and glory. Love for self leads mankind to sacrifice the future for the present. But selfless sacrifices made for others assure welfare of the future.

The parent that is led astray by the enemy to love and hunger after the material above all things puts his offspring at great risk of spiritual death. In his distraction, the parent often fails to shield the child from the pervasive darkness and encroaching evil that often overtake the young. The enemy of light seeks to corrupt the fruit of the tree. He seeks to corrupt the children so that the collective soul of humanity's future is bound with him in the earthen bowel. The earthen is miry clay that besmirches the soul to entrap all therein in consuming convulsions of envy and strife. It is a place that knows no peace for therein all thrive on blame and writhe in pain. Life therein is a helter-skelter existence that can neither sustain nor produce that which is stable or enduring. It is a joyless place of the unpleasant, regrettable, bitter and woeful endings.

The way of Christ is a better choice for it is upward bound and yields the good fruits of peace as well as life. Many are blind to Truth and have rejected the upward way that offers escape from the earthen. Such have rather chosen to follow the downward thrust that keeps mankind earthbound. As a result of that choice, many have sacrificed the future of the children to a gloomy doom for the temporary gains and wanted things of today's passing world. With a traumatic end in wait, this world is not meant to be mankind's final destination. It is but a transit point from where those deemed worthy will be lifted up for the journey to man's true home in the starry heights. Only those who have sincerely sought after and found Christ are deemed worthy for a passport and ride home.

Man will always be a worm crawling in the miry dust of

the earth until he finds Christ the gateway to Heaven. As long as he is determined to search by his wits and on own terms, man will be like Jacob and never find the gateway. The conversation in heavenly places that he desires is not of the mind and flesh but in the spirit. Mankind can only find the gateway that leads on to the starry when he realizes that it is futile and to his spiritual detriment to wrestle with God. The worm hole or the gateway to the heavenly that leads to the starry realm is Christ. Mankind has to search in Truth with love for God in order to have a chance of meeting up with Christ. Not all who catch a glimpse of Christ will meet up with him to board the flight home for many are called but a few are chosen. Those left out will be unwilling to let go of the world in order to meet up to Christ. However some will be willing to forego all to meet up with Christ to board for home. The seeker who has found Christ will forever pass in and out through him to find fresh pasture in pristine fields. This will always hold true as each age ends and another begins. He that is framed in spirit by the door posts of Christ has come into regeneration and will always bring new things out of old.

He that has met up with Christ has become part of true Israel and the living church. He has become a prince of God among men christened in light as a savior to model the way to eternal life for many others. The truth about Christ Jesus has already been told and published for all to know. Mankind has been adequately and sufficiently informed about the gift of grace through Christ. There are many alive today who have found and passed through the door of Christ to take spiritual flight into God's kingdom of light. Those are the truly faithful who have spiritually matured through grace to live under mercy in the kingdom of light. Sadly most men are yet to afford this divine portion and have no knowledge of the place beyond. They consider themselves as having made it on earth and sit pretty well. Such are the damned and already condemned who have sought after and found fool's gold to heart's fill. They have failed to realize that the earth is a dump that will always be recycled. They have failed to realize that true gold is only found in the place beyond.

The truth is that the earth is constantly being recycled by the non-wasting heavenly Father who searches everything so that nothing redeemable and salvageable is ever lost. Sooner or later a point of no return is reached when all the recyclables have been redeemed and the collectibles salvaged with nothing left but garbage. At that point of zero return with nothing of value left, the garbage is burnt so that a pristine landscape can emerge. The regeneration of the earth in the order of Heaven begins with the 'collectibles' who have passed through the door of Christ as the founding seedlings. The garbage that will be burnt is that which did not pass judgment and is of no use in the new age where Christ will reign.

The dutiful and faithful few who have chosen the upward way of Truth have chosen wisely. They have not only received and treasured the teachings of Christ at heart but have shared it as the bread of life to nourish others in anywhere they can. Through their diligent service in love, others have come to embrace the way of Christ to be led to find peace and new life within the Divine fold. Those that prove to be faithful in the light after Christ will always have a place reserved for them around the heavenly table to dine in divine light. Such will always dine in wisdom with Christ Jesus for they have come into the everlasting where the enduring and fulfilling is found. They have escaped the spiritual trap of the earthen to find shelter in the heavenly and starry. Those that are sheltered therein have come into faith rest to have a glow that shines forth out of their starry spirits. It is light borne of the anointing of God to crown every soul deemed worthy of Heaven by God. The light from within or sun evoked in righteousness serves as a beacon to show the blind true way before hope is lost.

The 'sun' of righteousness duly arises within the hearts who have found the door of life to find escape to the heavenly. The 'sun' of righteousness has arisen in the hearts of the faithful who have taken spiritual flight up to the source of all light. Such are the justified before God unto whom it has been appointed to save the unwary from the slaughter being visited on them by evil shepherds. There is an unmistakable illumination wherever true light has risen that helps the spiritually blind to see in better light. They that bear true light span the bridge between the old and the new that the uncertain soul must cross so that his heart can settle on God. Such are the faithful by whom the children are shielded from drowning in the pool of spiritual malaise that surrounds mankind everywhere.

Every bearer of true light is to show the young the way so that their minds may be sharpened and their ebbing strength renewed. The righteous before God is called to be a spiritual Father unto many so that the bond of faith between the 'fathers and sons' may once again be established. This is the bond that assures the showers of blessing on humanity from the heavenly without which the earth remains cursed. The curse of the earth is seeded in that which comes from below for it is weighty and stops the spirit of man from reaching for the heavenly. But that which is received from above uplifts man's soul to afford him gifts that satisfy his longings for fulfillment and peace.

He in whom the 'sun' of righteousness has risen is a very exalted spiritual being. He is specially anointed in the spirit of God to bring light into dark and hidden places so that many can escape from the darkness to find new life in Christ. True light sends the enemy to flight from wherever he has found a home. It shames the enemy and renders him powerless when he is withstood by the true light of Christ. Greater love is that which fuels true light so that the nature of all things can be truly known.

He that looks into the light borne of greater love in truth will receive insight into himself. He will see what he is doing wrong and where he is going astray. He will come to know what ails him and find healing thereby. The bearer of true light goes where the Father sends in love. He is led in the spirit of God to offer up prayers and receive answers for the children in the way. The child is one, whether he is young or old, who comes in trust and sincerity to seek answers and find healing through Christ. It takes the Holy Spirit to do the work of healing. The Holy Spirit is 'he' that is pleased or offended and not mankind. The trusting and sincere will never offend the Divine but the proud and presumptuous do. Therefore all whom the spirit of God will heal must be sincere and trust as obedient children do.

The spirit within the faithful matured in Christ never sleeps but remains awake at all hours night and day. The flesh oftentimes hinders the work of the spirit. Therefore the spirit is most effectual at night when the flesh is asleep and out of the way. Evil works flourish in the darkness of the night times. This is when the spirit of God is used by the heavenly Father to break the cords of bondage in answer to prayers. It is therefore important that prayers be offered to God without ceasing for every child at night before bedtime. The spirit of the Father works through the bearer of light at night when the forces of evil are at work. Evil exposed to the true light of Christ vacates those places where it has found a home. God remains unseen by the eyes of man but he can be perceived where the true light of Christ has risen in the heart to serve his will on earth. All who bear true light can 'see' God and are equipped to bring down the works of evil wherever encountered. Such that bear Truth in the light of Christ can take evil captive and cast it away where it can do little or no harm.

The bearer of light is a calf that has been reared to maturity in the stall of the Almighty Father. He is a sacred cow who exists for the meat of the spirit within and not for the meat of his flesh. It takes many seasons, at least seventeen years or more, to grow into full spiritual maturity in Christ and to be deemed righteous before God. The faithful that is matured in Christ has grown from grace as child to stand before God as a man under mercy. Christ has brought him home to be adopted by the heavenly Father into the family with a new name. The adopted has escaped death to become timeless for his spirit will live forever. Therefore he must devote his time on earth to do the heavenly Father's bidding above all things. Seventeen years is a long time to tarry for God but it is the blink of an eye in the scope of eternity. Eternity is creation's grand blessing and the golden crown of life. It is hard to let go of fame and fortune when one does not yet know that those two are impostors. Fame and fortune are rewards at best but blessings are far better for they never cease. Blessings never come with regrets and are passed forward to the next generation. Such are good everywhere and anytime. Eternal life and divine blessings, whoever has those can have anything that his heart desires.

Righteousness before God is not realized by the laws of Moses. The commandments of Moses are rudimentary laws which the believer can start with. The laws serve well to help mankind lead a moral and ethical life but to his surprise he will often find himself failing in one aspect of it or another. Obedience to the laws of Moses does not make man righteous. Righteousness before God is a far different matter. It pertains to those things that God wants the believer to do or not do. The secrets of the kingdom of God are communicated when the inner man is ready. As one matures in Christ, he is made aware of certain secrets of the kingdom so that he can be righteous before God.

Christ Jesus kept certain truths hidden from the masses but revealed them in private to the chosen. The secret things belong to God but those secrets communicated in spirit are done so that the faithful can remain obedient to the laws of God. Those are the statutes by which he will be shielded from the evil and corruption that surrounds him in the world. The faithful in light has to be shielded so that he can remain a clean vessel into which the father can pour a 'potion' of himself as the need arises. He who knows to observe the statutes appointed to him soon becomes the righteous in covenant with God. He will abide in the secret place of the Almighty God to remain in an everlasting covenant. Such has become a son of Heaven that can never be separated from the love of God.

Every son of the covenant has persevered in his spiritual journey to have Christ come to full spiritual maturity within him. He has become justified before God as well to be bestowed with righteousness. It is an exalted honor and he who is so blessed must not be ashamed to declare it. It is not self that the righteous declares but Christ within him. Unless the lamp is placed on a stand, many will not receive the benefits of its light. The declaration of Christ within is affirmed as God uses the son of covenant to answer the prayers of many. Everyone so exalted has been elected to serve a flock appointed for him within an earthly plot. The son of covenant lives a life of amazement but first he has to pass through the crucible of the world's rejection so that he can learn to remain humble. He is often persecuted for love of Truth and for walking on the path that pleases God and not men. He has to pass through the fire of the world's hatred before he can be baptized in spirit to be welcomed into the secret place.

The son of covenant lives as an instrument to receive from God through Christ and share with the willing so that his will is carried out on earth. The spirit of the enemy acts in disobedience to the will of God. But the spirit of Christ acts in obedience to his sovereign will. When the spirit of God speaks to the heart the faithful must obey for evil not to overwhelm humanity. It is righteousness fulfilled when mankind obeys God in all things and at all times. The power to destroy the works of evil on earth wherever such exist is the birthright of the sons. That birthright is the trump card that assures victory for them through Christ.

✓ The enemy is a determined foe who aims for the spiritual strangulation of mankind's offspring.

✓ The enemy aims to corrupt the children so that mankind's future is bound with him in the earthen.

✓ Mankind can never reconnect with God as long as he is determined to do it in his mind and flesh.

✓ The earth is recycled for the worthy to be salvaged so that the unworthy is burnt in a fire of judgment.

✓ The heavenly Father searches everything on earth so that nothing redeemable or salvageable is lost.

✓ The gifts received from above uplift man's soul and satisfy his longings for fulfillment and peace.

✓ The enemy is rendered powerless and shamed into oblivion when he is withstood by true light.

✓ The 'child' that looks in the mirror of Truth will receive insight into the man he is ordained to be.

✓ Though the heavenly Father remains unseen he can be perceived in the faithful who serve his will.

✓ God's elect is a sacred cow who exists for the meat of the spirit and not for the meat of his flesh.

✓ The faithful that remains a clean vessel will always be filled with a 'potion' of the divine.

✓ He that is privy to Divine will but acts not on it unwittingly serves the purposes of the enemy.

✓ The power to destroy evil wherever encountered is the birthright of the sons.

The voice of Truth echoes in love

Through every color and tongue

So mankind can know the Divine

Regardless of guise HE appears in

Chapter 6

OF TRUTH, LIGHT AND LOVE

God desires nothing more than to be in spiritual communion with his favorite creation man. Sadly man's sinful ways and pride make this communal fellowship with God impossible. Mankind needs to understand that his reconciliation with the heavenly Father rests on two unchangeable truths. Firstly, he must accept that all have sinned and come short of the glory of God. Secondly, he has to confess his sins and accept the sacrifice availed by grace through Christ as payment for sin in order to be reconciled with God. Though it sounds simple enough, yet mankind willfully refuses to accept the gift of grace readily. It is in man's nature to expect punishment and reprisal for every offence committed. He fails to recognize or accept that the sin nature is one area where he is powerless to do anything. He is powerless because spiritual payment is required to cleanse man of sin. Sinful man is not able to make this payment because he is spiritually dead. Yet he cannot become spiritually alive until payment is made.

Someone acceptable to God as a suitable sacrifice has to

make the spiritual payment in man's stead so that his dead spirit can awaken to life. The gift of new life is the noblest of all gifts and man can receive it through Christ. Christ Jesus has made the payment for sin so that all who believe in him as mankind's redeemer can have a chance of reconciliation with God. For true believers, the spirit within can be awakened to new life if that is the Divine will for such. God who searches the hearts of mankind knows their contents and intentions. God is the final arbiter and chooses whom he deems fit for awakening within to begin the journey of spiritual transformation that leads to him.

In order to walk faithfully on the path towards God, the awakened in spirit must continue to feed and live in accordance with Truth. Living in obedience to Truth helps to sustain the awakened spirit in the way of light on to full maturity in Christ. Living in the light of Truth through the teachings of Christ affords the divine essence to inspire and strengthen the spirit within the believer. The word of God that he feeds upon is the bread of life that will in time turn into spiritual meat within the believer as he matures in the way of light after Christ. It is for this reason that it is important for the believer to devote quality time to prayer and study of the word of Truth. The hour of prayer is the refueling stop for the spirit. It is the water break taken at the oasis of life by the weary traveler. The believer must drink regularly from the trough of the living water of the word else his nascent spirit will die of thirst. The young spirit, like all growing entities, must be regularly fed.

A more than necessary or inordinate focus on the things of the world is a great trap for many who seek after God. The hunger for earthly materials is a great inhibitor of man's spirit and faith in God. The love of the things of the world results in the neglect and rejection of God's way of light. The way of God and that of the world are opposed to each other. There will never be compromise between the two. God is faithful but very jealous. He leaves man with the choice to follow the way his heart desires. It is this choice determined solely by the desires and intentions of each man's heart that prescribes the spiritual path that he will take in life. For many the door to the heavenly Father will forever remain closed. But for some it will always be open to receive due welcome into his family because their hearts seek after righteousness.

Those who love Truth and seek after righteousness will be availed the light of God to direct their footsteps. They will be guided in that light to follow after Christ and will meet him in due season in accordance with God's will. God always makes accommodation for the spiritually ignorant to find redemption. For this reason, his Spirit will induce the man availed light to share with others in love so that such can begin to perceive as he does. The sight received in light is spiritual perception and it is a gift from the heavenly Father to some but not to all men. Many in the world lack this spiritual gift and so cast about oblivious of the Divine. They lack spiritual sight because they let the dictates of the world be the guide of their life. They that lack perception often regress into outer darkness where hopelessness abound and the dead or dying dwell.

The gift of spiritual sight is a very special gift. It is not to be taken lightly but must be cherished and treasured in the heart. He who has this gift is able to see the pitfalls and entrapments that the prince of darkness has dug all over the world. Spiritual sight is like a navigational instrument to guide the footsteps and aid the faithful believer in his earthly journey. The world is an obstacle course which must be navigated successfully to win the crown of eternal life reserved for the worthy by God. All start the race but only those guided in light and shielded in love by the unseen hand of God are successful at the end.

The prince of darkness has dug all manner of traps in his determination to stop as many as he can from completing the obstacle course of the world in victory. God on the other hand provides necessary navigational instruments and guidance tools to aid the faithful to complete the course. He waits anxiously and in earnest expectation for those appointed for victory in this light. He already knows how many will complete the course and so he spares no efforts to make sure that they do. The obstacle course of the world is definitely a maze but the eyes of God are always on the faithful to avail them light to direct their footsteps. And so every faithful believer whose eyes and heart are fixed on God will always be guided in true light.

Those deemed worthy by God are marked by a common

attribute. They are compassionate of heart and do not withhold mercy from the needy. Much has been given to them and the Father expects much in return from them. They have been prepared and equipped to act as the Father would if he were here on earth himself. The faithful believer that is used by God to carry out his will on earth is a divine proxy. He who has been chosen in this wise must open his heart to all for he has become a conduit for divine help to reach mankind and for goodness to abound. Such is one filled with essence of the Divine and must not shut off the stream of benevolence from flowing through him.

As the faithful fulfills his role and lives in accordance to Truth with love for God, he will be infused with the attributes of the Divine. He that has been infused with godly attributes can induce those same attributes or essence in all that sincerely embrace Truth. The godly in spirit can help seekers find healing and obtain release from the things that trouble them. They are God's anointed physicians, in the same wise as Christ Jesus, in that through them many will come to find answers for life's ailments. They that are endued with godly attributes are enthroned in grace and therefore have access into the preserve of the mercy wherein mankind's needs are met by the heavenly Father.

The faithful believer that has access into the preserve of mercy has been exalted into the place where all wishes are duly granted. The preserve of mercy is where all that are needed by the faithful are provided. It is the dispensary where the physician makes requisition for all that he needs to help make people and situations whole. Every physician in this wise has received the gift of insight and will be divinely endued with wisdom as needed. Such is exalted and will not see things as most men do but perceive from a higher plane. He sees from above and will therefore be circumspect in all matters. The circumspective in spirit is able to know what is needed, lacking or cluttering the way and can sort things out to make them better.

He that God has deemed to be worthy must use his gifts well and complete the mission ordained for him as the time is limited. Often the ordained mission is a lifelong calling and involves much sacrifice but God knows that. Therefore he has set a season for every faithful servant to come into faith rest after such has honored his calling. The burden of Christ does come to an end when the worthy before God have raised others worthy to serve God in light. It is all in accordance with God's will and mankind has no say in the matter. Being that the season appointed for those that serve God under the burden of Christ is limited, such must labor diligently to serve him well as the good shepherds appointed for the flock.

All who are not in fellowship with Christ are outside the will of God and in league with the prince of darkness. There is no neutrality in the battle of light against darkness for it has to be one or the other. The love of the world has blinded the faithless so that they have given room for darkness to thrive in their lives. In their willful blindness, such have led the unwary into the ditches of sin. The unwitting victims of sin have to be led back to the path of righteousness for God will not suffer the souls of those whom he has earmarked for redemption and predestined for salvation to suffer corruption. Every one unwittingly led into sin is appointed a 'savior' to come to his rescue in the light of Christ and only to such will the lost respond.

The Spirit that calls in love from within those matured in Christ is one that all those predestined for salvation had known from a long time ago in their distant past. It is the call of destiny that echoes ceaselessly and timelessly in the hearts of all who will come to be reconciled with God. Such are destined for spiritual transformation to become adopted into the divine household. They are led to pass through certain places, encounter certain people and do certain things during their earthly sojourn. It is at the meeting points of these places, people and things that the enemy has laid his traps of deception. It is at these entrapment points that the faith of the believer is tested and victory is wrought. It has all been programmed from the beginning of time by the heavenly Father.

Truth will always guide the faithful believer who has put his trust in God past every obstacle in his way through the light of Christ. Ways of escape will be availed to him to escape temptations as well as be shielded from the evil ploys of the enemy. He that has been so shielded and guided through Christ is called to be the guide to bring others from the darkness into light. He must respond to this calling for it is by such that he will come to know and be known in Heaven above as well as on earth below. He who responds well and is productive in this calling will be ushered deeper into the wellspring of the Divine. He will be the faithful laborer granted access into the purer and truer to duly realize the fullness of the riches of God.

The realm of the pure and true is the place of victorious living where God makes many miracles to come about. He that has tasted the pure and true will never be content with the glory that the world affords. He may have a taste of it but he will find the worldly to be unfulfilling and dissatisfactory. True fulfillment can only be realized in the fullness of time as the faithful fulfills the mission divinely destined for him through Christ. It is in the harvest field of Christ that the Father imparts his glory on the faithful for worthy service. Therefore the true laborer must get on with the task before him as the time appointed is limited. He that has been bestowed with divine glory is a son of light anointed to help true seekers after Christ realize hope of eternal life with the heavenly Father.

Whatever the son of light encounters along the way in his earthly path is foreknown. God therefore makes provision so he can be availed that needed to overcome problems and obstacles. Every son of light has three silver bullets given to him to handle the issues of life. His thoughts and wishes are like bullets that stream out to heavenly places to connect with the Father, the first born Son Jesus as well as the Spirit. They are used to summon help and to accomplish the desires of the heart. The christened will not comprehend the depth of that which has been poured into him initially. But he will come to understand the extent of the power that he is connected to as he passes through and overcomes many problems. The sharpness of every sword is only understood and appreciated by the many beasts slain with it on life's path. The words that the follower in light after Christ speaks constitute the sword. The silver bullets are only entrusted to those who have wielded the sword nobly. He that has the silver bullet need not speak much anymore for as he thinks in his heart, so it comes to pass. Yet he may not fully understand that he has come into unity with God whose wisdom is unsearchable and depths unfathomable. And so, he only scratches the surface of what is possible within the divine infinitude.

Every son of light will never encounter more than he can handle. Every trial that encounters is to show him a little more of what is possible through the heavenly Father. He that reaches out for more will find the light to get brighter and brighter. The temptations may get more challenging but every son has been given the Holy Ghost to inform him and the Holy Spirit to enable him in all things. God always accompanies the sons through life in truth, light and love.

It is companionship framed with goodness and mercy in abiding faith where the Father can never leave the son and nothing can separate from the eternity of divine love.

It is a promise made by the heavenly Father in love that his anointing will be with the faithful in goodness and mercy. He that has the anointing of the Divine will always be refreshed in light. The believer that faithfully walks in the light of Christ will always find refreshment even as he pours out himself in love to all who embrace Truth. When truth and light lead into the love that never ceases, life becomes glorified. Where life has becomes glorified, death is vanquished. For the faithful that have been found worthy by God, death is no longer the end of life's journey but the continuation of a glorious life in divine love. Glory belongs to God and things become glorified when he plays a decisive role in them. Such is what defines eternity for it is that realm where life is glorified through the warmth of love, light of Christ and power of God so death has no stake there. It is to join up with the Divine in the forever glory of eternity that the faithful labor and hope for.

✓ New life is a noble gift and mankind can receive such in love through the light of Christ.

✓ Truth affords the divine essence that the inner man draws inspiration and strength from.

✓ He who lets the dictates of the world be the guide of life will be blind and lack spiritual perception.

✓ Spiritual perception guides the footsteps of the faithful believer in his earthly journey through life.

✓ The faithful guided by the Divine is able to find his way through the maze of the world in victory.

✓ The compassionate and charitable are chosen by God to be conduits for divine gifts to the needy.

✓ The essence of divine living is manifested in things that are fulfilling, sustainable and enduring.

✓ The exalted in light know what is important or cluttering the way in any given situation.

✓ It is at the entrapment points laid down by the enemy that faith is tested and victory wrought.

✓ The faithful that is productive in his calling is ushered deeper into the wellspring of the Divine.

✓ Glory belongs to God and things become glorified when he plays a role in earthly endeavors.

Regeneration begins at point of escape

From the misguided and misgiven past

Tis much like the welcome face of dawn

A break that follows an unending night

Chapter 7

IN LIGHT AND WONDER

Every believer that matures in spirit through a faithful relationship with God and whose mind dwells on the uplifting things will come into a season of regeneration. The season of regeneration is the time of a new beginning in a believer's life when all which he touches will seem to turn into proverbial gold. This is when he will begin to do many things exceptionally well. This comes about from the ability to see and think from a divine perspective as well as having the aid of an unseen heavenly host. It is a season when the faithful believer is inspired in many ways to produce such works that shine before men to God's glory. It is a time when the greater and fuller light dawns in the life of the truly faithful in Christ so that they may serve God's will well on earth.

Regeneration begins at the point of total escape from the misguided and misgiven past. It is like the welcome break of dawn that follows a nightmarish night. The light of this new dawn is ideal for the believer to realize and nurture many spiritual gifts. Regeneration is ideal for the little seed with God in it. No other manner of seed will thrive under its judging and proving light. It is light that offers evidence that the spring of a grand awakening has finally arrived in the believer's life. Only those who have believed and kept faith with Truth in love awake to this light.

Such who have waited in hopeful belief become witnesses to all that God has promised mankind in love. They waited in hope for the time of fulfillment when the womb of the new dawn will open so that they can ascend to the higher and purer. They waited for the time of full manifestation when the power of God will be fully displayed to aid their endeavors. They waited for rebirth from the earthly to the heavenly. They waited for the new beginning destined for those who have found peace in God.

The faithful believer that comes into regeneration is a son of God equipped to do much good but the power to switch on the light for humanity's new age lies in a critical number of them. One son will chase a thousand but an adequate number of them will irreversibly change the world. God is always searching, choosing and adding sons to his divine household. The sons are chosen from all over the earth from different colors, countries, tribes and tongue. The tree of life produces a different manner of fruit each month and so a son to lighten the darkness is chosen even as the moon shows its full face every month.

A son is chosen and added to the count until a critical number that God only knows is reached.

It is Heaven's choice alone and mankind has no say in the choice of the sons except to yield his heart when God calls. The sons are paired in twos and work together as binary star systems. There is always a son that is in the lead and another that brings up the rear. The son that is in the lead reaches out and receives from the future. The son that brings up the rear keeps the past at bay so that what has been received from the future can be shielded from that which will corrupt it from the past. For instance the son that hears with certainty is paired with one who is fearless. Certainty makes for great vision and courage strong faith. The son that hears declares Truth with unequivocal certainty. He is the one that gives voice to that heard by faith which comes from beyond the heavenly throne to shine light on earth. On the other hand, the son that is fearless always finds a way to move the mountain that aims to shield the light and keep mankind in shadows or total darkness. Both sons make the pair that never gives up and perseveres to the end.

Both sons work together to conjure up the diamond spearhead that pierces through the flinty rock. It is a spearhead because it pierces the resistive to take man beyond the boundary of the hitherto known into that yet to be known. It is a diamond because it cuts across the whole world and through humanity to evoke the ever-increasing kingdom of Christ with nothing to stop it. Such is the spiritual dance of the matured or elder in faith with the yet to mature or younger. It is evoked and sustained by the heavenly dynamo that pulses endlessly through time. In the appointed season, the young becomes the elder and the elder is reborn into a young one. It is the Spirit of God that wills and acts through both to determine the due time to switch places. It is the ring of creation from which new life is spawn. It is death swallowed up by life or rather life mocking death.

The spiritual bond between the elder or matured and the younger or maturing is never broken once formed. This is the perennial dance of time in which the wonder of eternity is displayed. The emblem of this rebirth is the hourglass where one half empties into the other until it is turned over at fulfillment of time by divine mandate to begin a new spiritual sunrise. The lead changes within the spiritual bond at the moment of turning over when the younger becomes the elder and the latter is reborn as the young. The old has yielded to the new in this order of enlightenment through Christ.

There is momentary silence in Heaven when the hourglass is turned over but it is soon followed with great joy for it signals regeneration and dawn of the new age for the reborn in light. It is all by heaven's mandate and destiny's call. The new age is filled with peaceful hope and bubbles with magnanimous optimism. It is the grand awakening of humanity into its purified better. It is the ugly waking up to find itself beautifully transformed in the divine mirror. It is the saga of the ugly duckling turned into a beautiful swan that glides in majestic control through life. It unfolds from glory to more glory as time elapses. In this glorious dawn, everything gets better with the passage of time contrary to what the world's way offers mankind. It is the irrepressible combination of the elder and the younger in the bond of light that keeps the way open to make possible the spread of the kingdom of God.

Each son bears up the other so that the strength of one shores up the weakness of the other. It is two imperfect things mixed together with a pinch of divine salt to manifest that which is perfect. It is this search for the perfect that urges on the spread of light. It is this wisdom of the highest order that turns human weaknesses into marvelous strength much like carbon is transformed into diamond. The bond between the elder and the younger in spirit is the embodiment of that perfection much sought after but which still continues to elude humanity. It is that which always seems close but yet remains fleetingly out of reach for the most part. It is that which can only be realized through Christ.

Such unions of the elder and younger in the way of Christ

have been paired up and positioned by God all over the world. It is a thousand points of light coalescing into one great light. It is the dance of light to shame darkness into oblivion. It is the light of the flames that glows from the hearts of the sons joined in such unions that will blend together into the great dawn of humanity to bathe the world with the essence of Christ.

The essence of Christ is truth, light, love and the ever-lasting. The great dawn will be the realization of the reign of the kingdom of God on earth through the light of Christ. It is the moment of the twinkling of an eye when all shall be changed and death will be swallowed up by life. Such is the essence of regeneration and it is that which the whole creation has been hungering for. It is the better light by which mankind can cast his net in the world and have a good reward for his efforts without disappointments. He will be protected from disappointments because he casts in full light with an informed purpose and can therefore bring in the desired harvest every time to divine glory.

The faithful that has come into regeneration is a son of Heaven who has been well-prepared and equipped for the mission of Christ. He has become connected with the Divine mind to join the conversation in heavenly places which makes all things affordable and within reach. He has been given access through the power of prayer as the means to ask and receive without fail from Heaven. There is much power availed to the reborn in light but it can only be unlocked through petitions and requests made to God through prayers. It is power made available through Christ, with the Holy Spirit and for God's glory. It is power availed to the man who truly loves and gives due honor to God in all his undertakings. He that has been reborn in this light is a son who need not labor any more by his own devices for he can have much more accomplished in all areas of life through divine help. He has been given access and can summon a spiritual host to aid him unlike the faithless man who is left to labor alone in his own understanding.

In order to make the most effective use of the power of prayer, the petitioner must be mindful to desire those things that will please God. He has to earnestly invite the Holy Spirit to take the lead in all his endeavors and never fail to give God due thanks. It is not that God does not know what the son needs or craves praise. It is just that asking for it brings a measure of accountability into the relationship between creature and Creator. God grants the prayers of the faithful believer but the latter must live for the cause of love and goodness with charity as life's true calling. His motive must never be for personal gain but to serve humanity in love for by so doing will he be worthy before God to be richly blessed in many areas of life.

There are many who profess to follow after the footsteps of Christ Jesus who partake unworthily of grace availed thereby. For such the walk after Christ is for personal gain and not for the cause of love and goodness. There is an appointed time when grace runs its course. It marks the transition from spiritual childhood to manhood. When that time comes about, the faithful is ushered into the place of mercy before God. Mercy endures forever and it is for the few given to come into eternal life. The unworthy partaker of grace will never come into mercy for he will be stuck in spiritual immaturity for setting the divine feast to naught. He is one who has chosen filthy lucre and opted to serve the mammon of unrighteousness above God. The allure and abuse of grace has led many professed believers to unwittingly invite darkness into their lives.

Many who claim to walk in the way of light after Christ have become corrupted in spirit on account of addiction to grace. Grace is supposed to be a means to an end. Grace is transitional and not the end of spiritual quest. It is full spiritual maturity through grace on to mercy that is the desired end. In selfishly gouging themselves with grace, misguided believers have risked missing out on mercy which is enduring and salvation which is eternal. They have chosen to become bloated in the flesh but under nourished in spirit. Such have failed to understand that the flesh has to be pared for the spirit to flourish.

There is however an appointed season when grace is withheld from the unworthy. The end of the window of grace represents the beginning of pre-judgment within the body of fellowship that professes to walk in light after Christ. As the window of grace closes, the door of mercy is opened so that only those able to stand firmly in faith can walk in. The infirm spirit has no spiritual legs and cannot step into the realm of mercy for he cannot walk. The close of the window of grace is a season of spiritual self-examination divinely purposed to reset the heart so that the mind of the true seeker can refocus on God.

The believer that is enamored with and stuck in grace will be in an arrested spiritual development. There are many ways in which arrested spiritual growth manifests itself. The believer that is in arrested spiritual development cannot be weaned away from the milk of the word even though the season for him to be able to eat the meat of the word has come about. He is not able to study and understand the word of God by himself but still relies on another to teach him when he should be the one to teach others. He is not able to grow into a greater understanding of God but only regurgitates the old standards for he is not able to join the conversations in heavenly places. He cannot bear true testimony about the power of God for he has little experience of divine power that he can truthfully attest to.

The spirit of God is progressive and always brings new things out of the old. True faithfulness asks of the worthy believer to pour out self selflessly into others that lack so that they may come to know and see in true light. As due reward, the selfless sharer is always refilled with more and better from the divine largesse. The all-encompassing wisdom of God is beyond bounds and limits. Mortal man is only able to scratch the surface. Man's knowledge and experience with the Divine is ever unfolding. He that walks in true faithfulness with God will have a lifetime of amazing discoveries to uncover and unending experiences to testify about.

Of great importance and never to be overlooked is the fact that there are three dimensions of the Divine. In order for the believer to experience the Divine fully, it is necessary that he grows in three distinct areas of faith. The first is the area of the spirit which calls all believers to seek after God first before the things of the world take deep root to tie them down. All men can and do have experience with some measure of the spirit of the Divine. It comes in trickles as the voice of the conscience within that urges mankind to live by Truth and love others as he would himself. It flows in the faithful believer as the power that enables him to do the amazing to God's glory.

The second is the area of the knowledge and fulfillment of God's promises to man. The fulfillment of God's promises can be experienced through grace as the believer learns and lives in accordance with the teachings of Christ. Most believers are stuck in the second area which is the realm of grace and never grow beyond it. They are stuck there because it is the material benefit of grace that motivates them and not true love for Christ or the heavenly way. These are the ones who obtain the rewards but not the blessing that come with faith in God through Christ.

The seekers after rewards hoard material possessions along the way but are denied salvation and eternal life with the heavenly Father. They may have some measure of the divine experience through Christ but will never know fully to be received by the heavenly Father as sons. The third area of spiritual growth is that of knowledge of the heavenly Father which can only be experienced by the few who partake worthily of grace and grow in faith to stand upright before God in mercy. It is for such that the Holy Ghost is given to inform and the Holy Spirit to enable mightily. They receive all gifts with thankfulness to God and never fail to share what they receive with others in charity as love urges them.

Peace within and contentment without is the hallmark of the sharers and proof of their worthiness in grace. Because the worthy come in true love and not for gain, they duly grow to full spiritual maturity in Christ to be received by the Father as sons. Such are the ones given the passport of life to become the brethren of the Christ or 'Christ-Men' and divinely ordained to change humanity for better. They receive eternity's irreversible gift because they have passed judgment and proven to be real in the crucible of Christ. Such are the ones given to have the key of greater understanding and due access to Providence.

The season of judgment or self-examination within the fellowship of Christ serves faithful believers well. It helps to move them from the spiritual indolence of grace on to the spiritual vitality of mercy. Granted that not every believer has been ordained to come into the realm of mercy, it is important to note however that no one who truly desires a place therein is left behind. The unworthy that is stuck in grace is the goat that hides among the sheep of the flock to defile the divine feast of grace in greedy lust. The goats in the sheepfold always stick out when the rug of grace is removed. The unfaithful fall when the rug of grace is pulled back for there is no place left to hide under judgment but the faithful are left standing to bask in new knowledge and vision about God.

- ✓ There is a morning appointed for the true believer when he will see and know all things in a new light.
- ✓ There is always a son ordained to receive from the future and another to keep the past at bay.
- ✓ Hearts that are joined as one in love by Truth turn human weaknesses into marvelous strength.
- ✓ The matured in Spirit can have much accomplished for he has the help of a host of divine messengers.
- ✓ Spiritual rebirth must come about before man can come into the love and knowledge of the Divine.
- ✓ Peace within and contentment of soul without is a divine birthright and affirm spiritual worthiness.
- ✓ Total spiritual transformation courses through the indolence of grace on to the vitality of mercy.
- ✓ There is no hiding place under the judgment of light when the rug of grace is lifted.
- ✓ The faithful that passes judgment basks in the light of new knowledge and vision about God.

Mercy seeks in hope and rewards with life

For without it death roams about freely

It is the sunshine that warms the heart

As well the dew that waters thirsty souls

Chapter 8

FROM PERCH OF MERCY

God is not enamored with the many that pay him lip service by professing his name loudly. Rather his delight is to seek after the few who confess and serve him sincerely out of a pure heart. The spirit of God does not dwell in the noisome places where mankind often gathers to clamor for attention but rather in the quiet and peaceable places where man's heart is focused on him. A garden is a good representation of that quiet and peaceable place. A garden is where the divine purposes proceed in orderly conduct and nature displays herself in a lovely showcase. It is an ideal place for man to learn the unhurried directed pace of the divine way. A garden is devoid of the noisy interferences that often make it difficult for mankind to meditate and digest the meat of Truth.

The milk of the word of God is for the new and young beginner in the way of Christ. But to grow into spiritual maturity in light, the believer must be able to eat and digest the meat of Truth. Therefore a time comes in the spiritual life of the young believer, when he must become a man of faith. That time will never come unless he is able to put away childish things. The young in faith that is not able to tune out and turn off childish impulses will remain a believer in name only. He will never have faith that is rooted in experience with the Divine. Such can be easily misled for he is not anchored on the solid rock of the Almighty. Rather he will be given to look for the light of Christ everywhere except within himself. He will inevitably end either as an uncertain believer transfixed in fear or the non-believer that stampedes through life in hurried stumbling steps.

The believer who has grown from milk to eat and digest the meat of the word is the man of faith given to dwell on the spiritual housetop. The latter is for those who have been able to let go of the world so as to ascend upwards in spirit. It is from the vantage point of that housetop that the believer can be focused on God and availed due knowledge. It is from there that the believer is able to perceive that which is beyond the horizon to become a discerner of the future and the harbinger of the new. Because of his unique perspective, the dweller on the spiritual housetop is an agent of transformation who can change the human landscape for better. The spiritual housetop is the perch of mercy from which the good shepherd watches out dutifully for the sheep of the flock.

The spiritual housetop is a platform for prophecy from which things that loom on the horizon and lurk around the corner can be known. For that reason, the spiritual housetop is a desirable place for the believer to aspire for and to remain once up there. He who dwells there in spirit must not come down for he is one in communion with the Divine. He may be in the world but he is no longer of it. Rather all things that are in the house, that is to say the bottom dwellers mired in earthiness, must aspire to rise and join the spiritual dweller on the housetop.

All who dwell below and aspire for the spiritual housetop must not be concerned with the reproach of the world. It takes the battering and bruising that the world directs at the believer to dislodge the encumbering mud cake of the past that weighs down the spirit. The world's reproach is the toll that must be paid so that the spirit within can be free to ascend higher. It is a small token when compared to a future to be spent in company of the Divine as well as the goodness and mercy that comes to attend the ascendant spirit. It is the token that has to be paid to cross the bridge of destiny and escape from the tethers of the world into the freedom of hope. All believers must strive to ascend to the spiritual housetop for thereon can be found the only safe refuge from the overwhelming flood of malaise that unceasingly threatens to engulf mankind.

The faithful must cross the bridge of destiny in order to

escape the overwhelming dismal flood that licks at humanity's doorsteps. He must cross the bridge bearing his cross on his back. He may have to crawl on his hands and knees to get over that bridge in order to find refuge. He must cross the bridge for beyond it await safety and redemption. He that crosses the bridge will find the secure place of faith-rest where life is lived in penitent humility to God's glory, praise and honor. He that has found a place on the housetop is one justified before God. He is one called to receive from above and to share with those below so that they too may come to be lifted up as well.

He that dwells on the housetop is the bearer of messages that are too important to be withheld from humanity or compromised by the unfaithful. He is the voice of hope for the future through which salvation cries out. He is the last responder sent to the lost and floundering soul earmarked for redemption. He is given to speak Truth with an urgency that is often met with disbelieving indifference. Yet such is one who carries on for God and humanity though burdened by his duty nevertheless. The praise of mankind and the material benefits which can be gained from men is not the motivation for him. Rather he knows that the approval and love of the heavenly Father is a far better blessing to be desired above what the world offers.

The message of hope for mankind through Christ is too important not to be delivered and the Truth too revelatory not to be told. Most who profess to walk in light prefer the milk of the word. But no matter how sincere the milk, it is purposed to enable new born babies grow in the season of spiritual infancy. It takes the meat of the word to mature into the man of God. Spiritual babies reproduce babies after themselves but the spiritual man produces a son after God.

The truth about the demands of the way that leads to spiritual maturity is displeasing to most ears and hard to swallow for many. Therefore the Truth is often watered down for men's liking and mass appeal. It is in so doing that the purity of the message of the light of Christ becomes blunted so that many have come to be left in an arrested spiritual development. The true gospel is meat and the watered down is milk. The believer who is left in an arrested spiritual development is fearful, doubtful and unable to rise to the spiritual housetop. He will not mount up with the wings of the eagle for he will lack requisite faith. He will lack the spiritual strength and fortitude to forge ahead when trouble appears on the way. He will be one not given great vision and strong faith.

The faithful who is able to eat and digest the meat of the word is one that becomes duly matured in Christ. He will become transformed soon enough into a spiritual image of the Divine to become a member among those reborn in the light of Christ. But none of this can take place unless there is forgiveness of sins. Forgiveness of sins can only be obtained through the justification of God and it is for the believer willing to let go of all hurts and injustice rendered to him by men to receive. It is for this reason that wisdom declares that blessed are the merciful for they shall obtain mercy. The faithful that are justified before God become adopted into the divine household under mercy as the reborn in light whose sins are remembered no more.

Where forgiveness of sins has been obtained, the guilt of past sins no longer exists. There is a release and freedom of spirit that is experienced from the dissolution of guilt. It brings with it a new found peace that not only fosters the awakening but the flourishing of new life. It invigorates the spirit so that it can rise upwards to the utmost of the heavenly realm. It can be said then that the believer has become the faithful fitted with the wings of the eagle in divine glory. To be fitted and mounted up with the wings of the eagle affords the faithful believer the spiritual updraft to lift him up into the realm of mercy. In that realm all things can be known, can be obtained and can be sustained for mercy is comprehensive indeed.

He that dwells under mercy is able to stand before God for he has become known by the Father. He that can stand before God has become exalted in spirit and is privy to conversations in heavenly places as one given to serve divine purposes on earth. The faithful that is joined with

Divine in spirit must focus on the high and lofty things for the heavenly Father will grant his wishes duly. He will be given to ride upon the high places of the earth with the fullness of the blessings of Israel always at hand to attend his way. He will find that provision has been made along every path that he walks and that he will always have the knowledge as well as the wisdom necessary to produce pleasing outcomes always.

The wisdom that the merciful are bestowed with helps to heal the sick, make the wounded whole, repair the broken, refresh the thirsty and restore the dying. It is wisdom that is capable of endless wonders and such amazing works that make men give God due glory. The works accomplished when mankind is joined with the Divine shine so that the great power of God may be witnessed by all. It is with such divinely availed wisdom that the faithful becomes a breaker of new grounds given to do things in new ways that have never been done before. Such handiworks directed by the unseen guiding hand of divine wisdom may be likened to the honey comb that is sweet and fulfilling to the souls of men.

As mentioned earlier, he that must accomplish such works must remain on the spiritual housetop so that his mind can remain focused on the high things that bring glory to God and not be concerned with the worldly. The divinely inspired works that shine before men are done in the valley but the wisdom to do them comes from above. The faithful receive from exalted places in light in order to share with other men in the valley below in love. He that is grafted to share divine wisdom in this wise is in effect one that walks as Heaven's emissary among men. All who are such dwell in a place secure within the kingdom of God where they are immune from the evil in the world.

The kingdom of God is the new land fixed and secure where the way of light is the foundation. The kingdom of the world on the other hand is a turbulent sea of darkness that froths with uncertainty and wanton anger. Its foundation shifts with unexpected twists and turns that leave the misguided dazed with disappointed hopes. There are different and opposite sensibilities to living in either the kingdom of God or that of the world. The dwellers in the kingdom of God are guided in spirit to demonstrate the way of life within the divine fold. All such have been established under the mercy of God to live as model vessels chosen to exemplify kingdom life in the love and light of Christ. It is for this reason that they travel calmly on life's road for they have the assurance of spirit that all will be well for them through the earthly journey.

The kingdom of God is a place of demonstrating the power in the Truth that had been taught and received by the faithful at heart. It is a realm reserved for those who have received such Truth in good faith and live in accordance with its teaching. Such who dwell in this spiritual realm will begin to access the power of God to much effect. They will begin to appropriate a host of services through the Spirit of the most-high God. The faithful who have entered into that realm have ceased from laboring alone. All such handiworks that are ascribed to them are done through the power of the spirit of God. In that realm, all things are done in the greater light that precludes wanting, hurrying and wasting. All who dwell there are the good custodians who have learned to maintain what has been entrusted into their care with due diligence. Such take what is needed, use it for fruitful purposes and replace same in good stead so that all who are of good faith may share in its benefits to the glory of God.

To dwell in the kingdom of God is to live in the place of the endless cycle of divine blessing. It is the life lived where the guiding standards are according to the pattern and orderliness of heaven. For the faithful believer to be the good custodian who maintains what has been entrusted to him in diligent care, he has to be washed in soul and broiled in the fire of the spirit of Truth through Christ. The process of washing the soul prepares the faithful so that he can grow from grace unto mercy. The washing of the soul results from the material and personal choices made by the believer as he seeks after a reconnection with the Divine. The material and personal sacrifices made by the believer as he chooses God over the world serve to reset his mind towards God and pare down the contents of the earthly backpack that he carries to the bare essentials in order to streamline his life. Such streamlining helps to prepare and condition the mind and flesh so that man's spirit can focus better on the heavenly.

The washing of the soul works as an amplifier in the life of the believer so that the still small guiding voice of God can be clearly and loudly heard. It helps to bring the faithful to the doorstep of the Divine. The faithful must be willing to enter through that door and take a seat. He must be willing to commend his spirit into divine safe keeping and let God's will be done in his life. He must be willing to trust and join his will to that of the divine Father. He can never do better otherwise or get a better deal elsewhere. To enter through the door that separates from the worldly is the grand decision of faith. It is the choice that must be made if the believer desires to come into an everlasting bond with the heavenly Father. To enter through the door is to go all the way to full maturity in Christ so that the mortal can become the immortal remade in divine image.

✓ It is from the perch of the spiritual housetop that the eye of the spirit can be truly focused on God.

✓ The encumbering mud cake of the past has to be dislodged and washed off before the spirit can rise.

✓ The faithful that has received justification can petition and receive forgiveness for others that ask.

✓ There is a release and freedom of spirit obtained from the dissolution of guilt that fosters new life.

✓ The faithful that are joined with the Divine will be privy to conversations in heavenly places.

✓ The kingdom of the world shifts with twists and turns that leave many with disappointed hopes.

✓ The kingdom of God is a place that validates the power of the truth laden in the faithful heart.

✓ The 'shame of the cross' is the payment that declares that mankind has given his heart to God.

✓ The faithful divine vessel labors under the obscured self so that God may have the glory.

✓ The reborn in light is given to re-create the old where the new is always better than the former.

Amazing place where heaven and earth

Touch in the embrace and kiss of love

Tis where the good gifts are exchanged

Tween enduring faith and abiding love

Chapter 9

WHERE HEAVEN MEETS EARTH

Heaven is certainly a far-away place even as earth is very near and at hand for mankind. Yet there is a place where both heaven and earth meet in love. Man can reach out there through due praise, honor and acknowledgement of the goodness of God. It has been deemed as the place of joy unspeakable and praise is the key that lifts the soul up there. The believer that always has a song in his heart and whose voice has been tuned to sing God's praise will always walk in the sunshine of divine love. Psalms and spiritual songs are not for mindless entertainment or purposeless appeals to the flesh. Rather such are expressions of the believer's experiences in his faith walk that lend testimony to the goodness and abiding love of God. The psalms and spiritual songs speak about situations that the faithful believer has been through in his spiritual walk with God. Such expressions are in fact testimonies borne of spontaneous exuberance and unsolicited candor.

Praise and thanksgiving serve as sweet candy that the faithful believer offers up in love to the heavenly Father. They flow out of self-impulse from the wellspring of the believer's heart and attest to the abiding love of an unfailingly faithful God. They serve to validate God and affirm his goodness to all that trust. They are of much relevance and comfort to all who walk after the footsteps of Christ. The places and times may vary but the experiences expressed in the psalms and spiritual songs follow the same narrative. The psalms and spiritual songs extol the efficacy of grace, the enduring nature of mercy and the infallibility of God's words of promise. They sustain both the young believer whose muscles of faith are not yet firm as well as the matured believer as he finishes out his life's work and earthly walk in testament to redeeming glory.

The psalms and hymns are like camp songs for those whose spirits have joined the congregation of the heaven bound. There are the songs piped to the children in the market place which the wise must do well to heed and dance to. The songs frame the experiences of the faithful who has taken flight in spirit to the places beyond man's flesh. There are like postcards that fill the believer with much joy and comfort for there are reminders of the places that he has been to. They fill the hearts of those who have not been with encouragement and hope that they too will someday get to such places that the songs extol. They inspire those who have not been to trust and obey so that they too may in time be lifted up in spirit to the places where the songs speak about.

The true believer who has followed after the footsteps of Christ in faithfulness to full spiritual maturity can relate to where and about what each song speaks about. The songs are like growth rings in a tree that attest to the dreary winters and cheerful summers gone by. The faithful is a tree of righteousness that has passed through certain places at certain times to encounter certain situations on the ordained trail along which all of God's faithful walk. The songs therefore paint the same portrait of a benevolent Father who dutifully watches over the sons and daughters that he has sent out to tend his garden earth. Quite often they forget to do the job and wander off for a season but soon enough they heed the call to get back and carry on with the heavenly Father's business. It is in so doing that the redeemed bring much benefit to earth and give cause for much joy in heaven.

The believer is exhorted to sing from the heart with grace because doing so is refreshingly evocative. The psalms and spiritual songs bring up memories of the faithful goodness of God in times past and serve to reassure the believer about the future. God did not fail him in the past and will not fail him in the future. At times things may not look promising or seem to be falling apart but in the long run

God never fails to fulfill his promises to the faithful man. As a matter of fact, things may not turn out as originally expected and may take longer but it is always better in the end for the faithful believer when God is involved.

It takes grace in the heart woven into songs to remind the believer about that which protects and shields him from all his troubles. It reminds him that his survival and eventual victory will not be assured by his own hands but by the provident hand availed by the Divine. It is grace that sustains and establishes the faithful in his spiritual walk until he is able to walk before God in mercy. As he sings with grace in his heart more of God's anointing is poured out so that the faithful abounds fully in spirit. Grace keeps the believer humble and penitent for he is aware that there is an unseen hand there to protect him.

Songs remind the faithful partaker that he must strive to remain a clean vessel acceptable to be used by God for diligent service. He is reminded to make himself totally and readily available for this use. Songs remind that grace is to be used for the mutual benefit of all and not be abused through selfish greed. They also encourage the faithful man to serve humanity with his best at all times and need not worry for God will always multiply those things that are sincerely sacrificed on account of love and goodness. It is for these and other reasons that the free in spirit sing in praise to the Redeemer and Care-taker above.

The psalms and spiritual songs lift the spirit of the believer up to the place where heaven and earth embrace in the kiss of love. It is a place where gifts are exchanged. The faithful believer gives to Heaven from his heart. Heaven receives from such with much approval and replenishes same with the hidden treasure. The hidden treasure of Heaven is prescient knowledge and words of wisdom whispered from above into the heart of the faithful. It is for this reason that the sweet hours of songs, study and prayer are cherished by the heart that is truly after God.

Such times are often the golden moments when the precious is received by the open and waiting heart. Each word of knowledge given and received is a key to help unlock the mystifying in life. The words bring insightful knowledge about the issues that bedevil life on earth. The enemy seeks to frustrate the believer in the small details of life so that he may lose sight of the big picture that God is working out for him. The key to defeating the enemy lies in the daily word of comforting Truth whispered in those moments when the faithful believer brings his hurting heart to offer up thanksgiving in songs and prayer to his heavenly Father in love. It is then that the divine healing balm is availed to soothe the aching heart.

The words of scripture contain pictures that are not readily discernible except by the matured in spirit. Some elements of the words of scriptures are addressed to the intellect but most are not. He that depends on his intellect to discern the words of scriptures will never get the full picture. The knowledge and wisdom that are concealed within the scriptures can only be 'figured' out by man through the understanding of the spirit. The 'truths' concealed within the words of scripture are elements of the spirit that reveal themselves only to the noble souls that have become worthy to stand before God in mercy. Such elements are pictures purposely disguised within the scriptures by the Divine to baffle the pretentious and presumptuous pithy mind of faithless man. On the other hand, such elements progressively reveal themselves to the true seeker who comes in humility and with sincere desire to know so that he can serve God to the utmost. They reveal themselves not before but after man has passed through the experiences that such truths portray.

In a way, the words of scriptures are written backwards so that it is only when viewed through the lens of experience that they come into sharp focus to be truly understood. It is only when the teachings of scripture become a lifestyle that their validity can be known to the faithful. It is only by faithful living and through hindsight borne of experience that they can become fully understood. The Truth within the scriptures cannot be surmised. Rather the scriptures should be seen as a jig-saw puzzle that can only be put together when certain keys are known. Only when the keys are known does the orderliness and harmony therein surface. The experiences which afford the believer the keys demand a lot of patience and trust to come by.

It is never easy to learn man's earthly languages even as lowly as such are. The scriptures speak a much higher and purer language that can begin to be figured out only after the mind has been washed and conditioned in Truth. It is quite a tall order to wash man's mind that is steeped in the consciousness of the world in the purifying dew of Truth. It is that difficult because the world prefers and revolves around the false white-washed as Truth. The world has become accustomed to the deceitful rubbish of the white-washed and so it becomes quite a feat to keep mankind from returning to the muddy. However God in his mysterious way does make it possible for the faithful to remain washed in Truth even in a world awash in the false that defiles many. God will cause those that he has earmarked to hear and keep Truth safely guarded at heart even in the midst of a muddy and deceitful world.

There is the world that mankind knows and lives in. Then there are the worlds of the macro universe beyond. There is also the world of the miniscule or the micro universe. In every world known and yet unknown, the same principles of orderliness and harmony hidden in the scriptures hold forth. The key that unlocks the scriptures is the same that also unlocks every other world. The over-riding Truth hidden within the scriptures is the same upon which the universe is founded. The governing order is faithfulness to Truth or that proven by time to be ever true. The same faithfulness to Truth is found in the least as well as the greatest in all things. Scale and size do not change this overriding Truth. He that is faithful to Truth is entrusted with the key of knowledge that unlocks all. He that is faithful to the true will have orderliness and harmony as governors in life. Such can re-create and transform a plot of land on earth to reflect the order and harmony in the universe. The faithful believer who is able to do that can create an earthly paradise where man and God can commune in spirit to nourish each other in abiding love.

The paradise that the faithful believer creates in his earthly plot is a reflection of the spirit that dwells within him. It is the same mind that created the universe working through him to create a little heaven on earth both within in his inner man and without in his estate. Heaven on earth is that paradise where God communes with man in spirit and speaks with him in nuggets of Truth. The faithful that has been entrusted with the key of knowledge will be connected to the source of all wisdom. All who come into the plot of paradise on earth created by such a faithful one will sense a divine presence in its midst. All who come in there will begin to hunger for God. All who come in there in good hope will receive healing and enlightenment. Such will receive the good gifts concealed therein for the true and humble seeker to find.

The faithful that has been entrusted with the key of knowledge lives his life on earth in a kingdom parallel to that of the world. He keeps faith with God on the 'strait' and narrow path even as the world rushes by on the broad and hurried way. Oftentimes he has to venture into the kingdom of the world for that is where the lost are to be found. The lost sheep of the Father's flock have to be searched for and rescued from the kingdom of the world. Each time that the faithful one ventures there, he must pass through the opposing streams of the upward bound way of God and the downward thrust of the world.

This medium of contending opposites is a sort of tornado alley. It is a very stormy place but the faithful are shielded by the golden armor of Truth and divine love. Only the strong of faith that have been chosen by God for this mission can pass back and forth through the alley without being wrecked. Only the strong of faith with spiritual vision can crisscross this alley without compromising his integrity and faith. This medium of contention is a cauldron borne of conflicting passions that would shear and tear apart the hearts that have not been sanctified in Truth.

God always take care of the faithful as he makes his forays into the kingdom of the world so that its' rising waters will not overwhelm him. Such that is shielded and sanctified by Truth becomes an intrepid vessel used by God to demonstrate his divine power and love for mankind. The heavenly Father uses the intrepid vessel on those certain days marked in his divine calendar to shame the forces of darkness into submission and show that he is ever in control of the world.

The intrepid vessel can never be sunk as 'he' sails through the stormy and battering sea of the world. Such may not be massive but it has been optimally configured to weather all storms. God often uses the things deemed little and inconsequential by man to demonstrate his power. The intrepid vessel is a representative model for all things driven by the divine wind of the Spirit of God. The divine wind will always favor the intrepid vessel so that it remains unsinkable in every circumstance and situation that it encounters. The intrepid one may encounter many storms in life but God always sees him who is on an ordained mission through. The intrepid vessel always has new testimonies to give about God's unfailing faithfulness and therefore new songs to sing in accordance.

✓ The believer with a song in heart and voice tuned to sing God's praise will walk in sunshine of love.

✓ The psalms and spiritual songs give the believer hope for they testify about God's goodness to man.

✓ Songs paint the portrait of a Father who loves the sons that he has sent to tend garden-earth.

✓ Psalms and spiritual songs serve to reassure the believer so that he may serve God with his best.

✓ Grace reminds that there is an unseen hand that controls all and protects humanity in love.

✓ The psalms and spiritual songs uplift the spirit to the place where heaven and earth embrace in love.

✓ Truth is wisely disguised to baffle the pretentious and presumptuous mind of faithless man.

✓ Scriptures speak a language understood after the mind has been washed and conditioned in Truth.

✓ The orderliness and harmony hidden in the scriptures hold forth and governs all in creation.

The soul that's in communion with God

Is an extension of the Divine on earth

And conduit for those things that flow

From Heaven above to mankind below

Chapter 10

A NETWORK OF HOPE

The believer that is fully matured in Christ has become a son of Heaven who is connected to the universal mind of God. The son that is so connected functions more or less like a personal computer. He is connected, along with a host of other personal computers that are his sons as well, to a supercomputer God. The Holy Spirit makes available the power that energizes the system while the Holy Ghost affords the information shared within. Each son of God is given a new name which can be likened as the user identification into the network. All knowledge and needed help on how to do all things can be accessed through this network that links all the faithful that have been received into God's divine household. This is the living church of Christ and the commonwealth of the spirits of just men being perfected within the divine fold.

The sons of God have crossed the threshold from the short comings of the earthly experience into the perfecting womb of the divine experience. It is a living network akin to a beehive where all thoughts and minds blend together spiritually in a common will that serves God's divine purposes. The foremost task that each son is charged with is to seek out those that are still lost in the world who have been earmarked for salvation. It is the primary mission of the sons to find these erstwhile lost brothers and show them the way back to the heavenly homestead.

The lost ones are the square pegs trying so hard to fit into the round hole of the world. They are often oblivious of the fact that they are not of the same ilk as others who have not been earmarked for salvation. Many are the vessels of wrath but few are the vessels of mercy. It takes someone of their own ilk to remind those earmarked about the rich heritage and special privileges reserved for them within God's kingdom. It takes the son that knows how to strike up the familiar but long faded tune of old glory to lead each lost one back to the heavenly Father. The faithful who lives to help redeem the lost brother in this way will earn his heavenly stripes and divine wings.

Each son of God is charged to be an impartial judge that uses the golden rule as his standard but given to also temper justice with mercy in his dealings with mankind. He knows to be restrained as he passes judgment for all have sinned and come short of glory. He knows that there is not one good man except the heavenly Father who is perfect in every way. It is then incumbent on the sons not to rush to condemn others but to model the upward way and seek forgiveness for transgressors the best he can. Many men transgress because they do not yet know. Therefore hope should always be held out that the transgressor will come to see in better light and change his ways soon enough.

The sons of God are not readily known for who they are and what they represent. But In the course of time they come to be known for the light within them cannot be hidden. They speak with great insight into the affairs of men and future of mankind from a place beyond the commonplace. They are able to see around corners and beyond the horizon. They speak from a place of certain knowledge to bring divine light into the hidden and dark corners of men's hearts. Such words that they speak out are like arrows of Truth that pierce into hearts where sin lurks and guilt resides. The sinful heart that welcomes such Truth is led to change ways and find relief from the oppression of sin. But he that rejects same will have no hope left for redemption in this life.

The sons collectively represent man's last chance of redemption before humanity's great upheaval. Each son has been prepared to speak Truth to enlighten men's darkened hearts. The sons live as they speak as failure to do so bring them into the Father's judgment. Judgment does indeed begin within the household of God for the sword that each son carries cuts both ways. The honor of carrying the sword is reserved for the faithful few that are truly pure of heart and noble of soul. They live to please the heavenly Father and will go to any length to obey his divine will.

Each son is bestowed with divine anointing through Christ to teach Truth so that others may come to know in the light, knowledge and wisdom of God. He that has been bestowed with divine anointing is called to serve other men as God's elect on earth. His anointing is a gift from God for the benefit of humanity. It takes fortitude, wisdom and endurance to serve in this light. Therefore he that is bestowed with such anointing must seek for wisdom, vision and strong faith so as to be fruitful in his calling. Such must maintain his spiritual integrity so that no dead flies can be found in the oil of his anointing. He must remain suitably armored and make no room for the things that are displeasing in the eyes of the Father. Such mar the anointing to invite corruption and defile the spirit.

The sons constitute the Father's elite forces on earth who are informed via the Holy Ghost about where to direct their attention and mass their efforts. They are the agents being used to save the last remnant of humanity earmarked for salvation before judgment's bell tolls last. Heaven makes earthly appointments for the sons and they rally to the cause as summoned. As a result, it is their collective prayers and endeavors as guided by the Father's will that serves as the impetus to change the humanity for better. They are the gardeners of new Eden that use the power of prayer as their gardening tools to help those who love God but are choked in their hearts by the cares and worries of the world. The sons speak in little tweets of measured words but that which they speak must be received and welcomed to heart. They speak about what must be done now in a spirit of urgency that befits the times to wherever the hope of salvation yet remains. It should be noted that the sons can never be sent to those who have committed sins unto death for God is not wasteful. The latter are the truly lost who having had some experience of the Divine continue to revel in worldliness and deny the reality of God's existence.

There is a time of divine appointment ordained for all humanity. Divine appointments need to be heeded and kept. The time may be different for each but everyone on earth is given a chance to have a glimpse of the Divine. The appointed season is when God is near and can be readily experienced by those that sincerely seek to know. Such is an opportunity not to be wasted for it may never come again. It is a season when the inaudible voice of God can be easily and clearly heard. Mankind's response to that voice is a significant first step towards spiritual rehabilitation and must be obeyed when once heard in the heart. The voice that is heard always pleads with the receiver to heed the words of Truth as scripture spells out and God's commands dictate. God avails wisdom to the ready but true understanding comes with obedience to the words imparted to the hearer. He who hears and heeds will honor the hour of his visitation to his great gain. In due season, he will come to find his place within God's fold and be useful for the work of the kingdom on earth.

Those who hear and heed Heaven's inaudible yet timely call do become the building blocks of the kingdom and the vessels favored for mighty use by God. Every believer that has become a chosen vessel favored for the work of the kingdom will have the doors of Providence always open to meet his needs. The goodness and mercy of God will follow him always so that he will receive as he asks. He will knock and have the doors of opportunity opened to him as he serves the Divine will. He that has been chosen in this wise will know what to ask for and always receive the wherewithal needed to fulfill the calling.

- ✓ The faithful believer that has become a son of light is connected to the universal mind of God.
- ✓ The divine urge blends all thoughts and minds into a common will to serve God's divine purposes.
- ✓ It takes someone of the same spiritual ilk to rescue the erstwhile lost soul earmarked for redemption.
- ✓ Each son is a judge given to use the standard of the golden rule and the restraining hand of mercy.
- ✓ The honor of carrying the sword of Truth is reserved for the noble in spirit justified before God.
- ✓ The collective impetus of the wishes and prayers of the sons changes the human landscape.
- ✓ Knowledge is availed to those ready to receive but true understanding comes with obedience.
- ✓ The fisher of men is motivated by love that seeks to bring hope and restoration into man's existence.
- ✓ The sons of light find contentment on account of the goodness and mercy that follow them.

Wisdom that truly speaks to the heart

Changes not in tune or tone to please

But spirit that beguiles and misleads

Always changes pitch to suit the sale

Chapter 11

IN STEPS OF MERCY

The sons of God are given to walk under an illumination that endues them with the knowledge needed for victorious living on earth. All that each son needs to know is made known to him so that he is able to take assured and certain steps within divine will. The sons know to chase not after the transient but the enduring in life. For that reason, every son is given to take purposeful steps as one who is a model through whom God demonstrates his goodness to mankind. Many will come to believe, change their sinful ways and begin new lives through contact with the sons for it has been given to them to draw men to the heavenly way. They are able to do so not by their power or might but in the spirit of God which operates mightily through them to do the marvelous.

The sons know to be thankful for life's blessing and to remain vessels worthy of use by the heavenly Father. They also know that they have been empowered to accomplish much on earth through petitions and prayer. They can pray for forgiveness of sins and bring about healing in those that embrace Truth through Christ. Wherever the sons are well-received, much good comes about therein for goodness and mercy will attend there. Their prayer of earnest entreaty to God is given to make much available to those that embrace Truth. Each son has been elected both to offer up sacrifices and to receive blessings from the Father on behalf of humanity. Therefore each son is called to keep the doors of his heart open and live with compassion for all. It is within their hearts that the Spirit of God searches in order to ascertain what burdens are laid there so as to attend to those needs for the Father will not let his elect sons suffer needlessly.

As each son gets under the burden of another, the Divine spirit comes to buttress him. In this way, the sons appropriate God's divine power to help others. As the Spirit of the Father searches and ascertains what burdens each son, intercession is made to alleviate those problems. The heavenly Father always makes provision to meet the needs of the sons and those that embrace them. Therefore each son is called to set his heart on the things that please God so that the lovely worthy of good report may always abound through him. He is called to remain a clean vessel that is willing and ever-ready to serve God's purpose on earth. This is the reasonable service which affirms the elect sons and for which they have been prepared.

Each son of God is a vessel of mercy that must remain merciful towards humanity. He must not harbor resentments or dwell on past hurts. It must be so in order that the goodness and tender mercies of God may continue to follow him. Nothing must choke the channel of mercy for it must remain a freeway of light, love and life. The channel of mercy is the highway of the free in spirit who have overcome the world and given to ride in the high places where only few can venture. Worries, cares, grievances, resentments, grumblings, anger, envy and such emotional malware slowly but surely drag down the spirit into a stall. The stalled spirit cannot ascend and has no place on the highway of the free. He that harbors such a spirit cannot ride on the high places but must return to the low places of the earth as one who has vacated the place of honor that was appointed for him.

The measure of the spirit of each man is adversely affected by the resentments that he harbors from the past. The past is always marred and far from perfect but the future holds the promise of perfection. He that must stand in the congregation of the mighty must bid farewell to the imperfect past. He must bid farewell to the dark night of his past life so that he can wake up in the dawn of the new. Each son must forgive all in mercy for by him will the blessing of the latter rain and the tender mercies of God reach others. Wisdom declares that the blessed are the merciful for they have been given to obtain mercy. Mercy is akin to the cycle of rain. It benefits both those deemed as 'good' by men as well as the wicked. The sons live by the golden rule so as to model for both the 'good' and the wicked how things should be done on earth. It is through the enlightenment implicit in the golden rule by which they live that many come to see each other as creatures of same Creator. Many either do not know or are not sure about the heavenly way and so the few who know must demonstrate the way so others can follow.

The sons of God are called to model the way of mercy. There are no constraints or strings attached to mercy. Mercy is not constrained but flows freely with no demands attached for it is a divine gift. Mercy rejects the notion of superiority but makes ample accommodation for importunity. It seeks no rewards or accolades. It only requests to be received and shared as necessary with thanksgiving to God. It begs that hearts be opened to light and love but be closed to darkness and hatred. Mercy is indeed the last hope for beyond it is despair. Even the wicked man knows in his heart when mercy has reached him. Such is the power of the gift of mercy that it has led many wicked men to change their evil ways to seek after the Divine.

Within the core of mercy is found the goodness that covers and hides a multitude of sins as well as saves souls. The rain drop of mercy is the precursor and lifeblood of regeneration whereby the dying and broken down receive new life. The sons of mercy live by the understanding that God is in control and knows what is best for mankind in every situation. They know that God is a merciful, long-suffering, non-hasting and non-wasteful Father whose good plans for humanity are often hindered by man's impatient ways.

Many do not yet fully understand the divine way for such is much higher than mankind's. Each son must be merciful towards all for he has been called to live by a way that is higher than those of his fellows. He must ride the heavenly highway where the clouds of mercy form so that he can draw from there to be a fountain of living water for famished souls below. The exercise of mercy towards all brings the faithful believer nearer and closer to the heart of God where the fullness of divine riches is at hand. The place near to God's heart is where to receive knowledge as well as gifts to be shared in love.

The faithful believer that has come to the place close to the divine heart is under the greater divine illumination. Therefore he will have a fuller and better understanding of the Holy Scriptures. Being now in God's greater light, he is able to see the harmony in the scriptures and the veracity of its message. On a personal level, he will begin to see his life mirrored in the characters, places and events described in the scripture narratives. He will come to understand that the book of scriptures is indeed written to guide him through life. It is this understanding that enables the merciful one to settle in the place that God has reserved for him in his kingdom much as a star settles into the place ordained for it in the heavenly expanse.

The path that the faithful believer walks in life may seem to be winding and constraining but it leads the wanderer back to the heart of the Father. The heart of the Father is the fountain of life. In contrast the broad and hurried way of the world leads to the heart of darkness and death. The heart that has been led back to the Father beats in harmony with the Divine. A heart that beats like the heavenly Father's yields a mind that mimics that of the Divine. Such a heart with such a mind will be entrusted with the true riches of Heaven. Such a heart with such a mind equates to that of Christ. Such a heart with such a mind can indeed do all things with the Holy Spirit and to God's glory.

Only a few do come to know the place close to the heart of God for many are called but only a few are chosen. The few that get near are pure of heart and follow after Christ in the light of Truth. They are always willing to trust God, believe his words and pay the price for that trust for they know that they will gain the better in the long term. They are the ones despised and rejected but who walk alone regardless for they know where they are going. They are the ones crucified for love of God but who find new life through Christ. It is for them that the best has been saved for last with mercy as due inheritance.

The faithful who come close to the divine heart as well as their offspring will come to be established in righteousness through mercy. They will bring up their children with knowledge of the veiled truths upon which goodness and mercy bind themselves so that such will be like pleasurable wine to lift up their hearts in old age. All those who are established in righteousness do come into the season of restoration where the spirit of the Father is re-united with those of the children. Wisdom declares that all who come into that season will be rid and delivered from the hand of strange children whose mouths speak vanity and whose right hand is that of falsehood. Rather the sons of the righteousness will become as plants grown up in their youth to reflect the father's image and their daughters as corner-stones polished with divine attributes.

It is on this basis that the kingdom of God is founded. It is appointed for those that fear God and walk in light after Christ. It is the blessing promised in love for the man who has reverence for the Divine. All who think as the Father thinks and acts as he urges become his true children. The latter will begin to see the Father as he really is. They will find him to be an all- loving, all-knowing and all-merciful one that has their best interest at heart. This is when they will be led in spirit to become more and more like him. It is in this manner that the child becomes a man that has been remade in the likeness of the Father to enter a season of restoration and be held up as a standard for all to see.

In effect each son borne of mercy will becomes a branch of the tree of righteousness that is continuously pruned to produce even more good fruits. Each pruning season concludes with the son positioned to recreate that which he had produced on a small scale hitherto on a far grander scale. The first cycle of divine harvest is small and takes few hands to manage but the cycle that follows is always grand and requires more hands. Such is the progressive nature of the tree of righteousness in that it faithfully shows forth more branches in the passage of time. It is all by God's doing as part of that ever-lasting kingdom of peace and light of whose increase there shall be no end. It is all framed within the mosaic of eternity where all who are called must play their pre-destined part to God's glory.

- ✓ Many will change their ways and begin new lives in light through contact with the sons of God.
- ✓ Much good comes about wherever the sons of light are received for goodness and mercy follows them.
- ✓ The spirit of God searches to ascertain the burdens of the faithful in order to alleviate those needs.
- ✓ Each son of God is a vessel of mercy that must remain merciful towards all both good and bad.
- ✓ The measure of the spirit of each man is adversely affected by the resentments that he harbors.
- ✓ Mercy rejects the notion of superiority but makes accommodation for man's importunity.
- ✓ The abode of mercy is a place from which to know and receive as well as to share in thanksgiving.
- ✓ The matured under divine illumination will have a fuller and better understanding of all things.
- ✓ The path that the faithful walks is winding and constraining but it leads to the divine heart.
- ✓ Only a few come to know the realm close to the heart of God for many are called but a few chosen.

Light will find the young not saddled with age

Who is noble of soul and worthy to be trusted

For the way of wisdom is not to discriminate

But to seek for suitable and welcoming hearts

Chapter 12

OFFSPRING OF WISDOM

The Divine spirit is not static but remains ever dynamic. 'He' abounds and increases within the faithful believer to impact many areas of life. The fact that the faithful has come to full spiritual transformation does not mean that he has become 'perfect'. He is still growing spiritually day by day in different ways and many areas as the Divine directs him within. No one is ever perfect but God. The heavenly Father is an infinite God who has no limits. The infinite is unfathomable, unsearchable and fully unknowable. The infinite beckons ahead and the faithful can come close enough to it through the divine perfecting process. It is this desire to meet up with the Divine, which resonates strongly within faithful hearts and less so within the faithless that propels the spread of light.

The perfecting agent is the Holy Ghost that speaks to the man of God so that he may be duly informed and well prepared along life's path. The matured in spirit is endued with prescient knowledge by the Holy Ghost. He is fed with timely information from the throne of the heavenly Father about the important things to pay attention to in life. Such is availed insider information about the important in life for it seems as though a little bird whispers into his mind to brief him. He is fed the data that he needs in order to live in harmony within and with all around him. In effect, he receives constant tweets and updates from the dove of the Holy Ghost given from above. The latter speaks little but there is much said in those few words to the benefit of those tuned to hear 'Him'. It is for this reason that it is not possible for the sons or those spiritually in tune with the Divine to be deceived for they are availed pertinent information via the Holy Ghost.

Having been reborn in light, every son is free from the guilt of past sins and given to forgive all as well. As he forgives those who wrong him, both the memory and the associated guilt of his past sins fade away. He will cease to feel guilty for he has indeed become new in the light of Christ and justified before God. The new man is separate and freed from the old man of sin and guilt. He is one able to stand erect before God for he has been resurrected to sin no more. He has been given new life in order to serve God's divine will. He has become redeemed through Christ and will be kept or saved by God if he proves worthy.

The redeeming love of God availed through Christ is the

constant refrain and ever-lasting song of the faithful that has found new life. Such cannot help but bear faithful witness to what divine power avails mankind through love. All men have heard or know about God's promise of new life by grace through faith at this time. But sadly, the priceless offered in love is often ignored or dismissed by many as mere fairy tale. Such choose to join and follow the faithless throng of humanity that has no experience of the Divine. They make the popular but wrong choice of going with the crowd instead of listening to the voice of Truth within. They fear the ridicule of the world and neglect that which they know in their hearts to be true.

The truth is that God in his wisdom and mercy has infused humanity with some essence of the Divine. He has also left instructions on how mankind, if he so desires, can reconnect fully with his Creator. To God's glory many have heeded the Truth which gently tugs at the heart of every man and yielded to the divine urge. Such have left the way of the world that leads into further estrangement and turned to the way that leads back home to the Father of all. Through belief, trust, patience and commitment, they have followed the light of Christ to be guided back into the divine reality. God has become real to them as he now speaks and touches them through the heart. These are the ones who have come to know that all which the Heavenly Father speaks into the faithful heart proves to be timely and unfailingly true always.

The heavenly Father is ever faithful in fulfilling his promises to the faithful that walk on the righteous path. The pathway to God runs contrary to that of the world. Therefore to seek God in the world is to look for the living among the dead. He that runs with the 'Gedarene' herd of the in-crowd will sleep in the tomb. But he that walks towards the Divine in trust will find new life through Christ. The pathway that leads to the Father is the path less travelled. On that path the traveler may seem to walk alone but he is never really alone for he travels in the company of unseen messengers that guide, teach and encourage him. The seemingly lonely pathway leads to the mountaintop where the hidden truths lost in the mist of time crystallize and can be known. It is where night turns to day and space blends with time. It is the vortex of the creative impetus that wants not, hurries not and wastes not. Up there is the nursery of the perfect things where simplicity and orderliness attend as midwives. It is the exalted place out of which echoes the wisdom of all ages and from which the purified spirits can glimpse forwards and backwards in time as events unfold.

All who can ascend in spirit to the exalted heights have overcome the world. Eternity with the divine Father has been appointed for those who have overcome the world. Such are the ones worthy of the passport of life which grants man access to the realm of no limitations and infinite possibilities where the disciple can go further to do more than his master. But yet, it is a place where the disciple can never be above his master for the latter is in him always. The master takes the disciple along to guide him in the way so that the worthy for whom it is appointed can mature fully in light. He that has become matured must then take the old master along as the master took him along a long time ago. It is the undying reality of eternity and the saga of lives resurrected in Christ. The master dies but lives on within the worthy disciple as spiritual fathers and sons within the divine fraternal fold.

The spiritual fathers and sons do walk together in light as one as all good sons must do with their fathers. They walk together in the halls of wisdom as curators of humanity's collective goodness and redeeming grace. Their whispered voices of Truth blend together with those of the sages of the ages gone before them. Their whispered truths echo back to those seekers who follow in their footsteps. They cause all things to glow in their wake for those things that are pure do glow from within and enlighten the trail for those who follow after them. The faithful counted worthy of wisdom is able to ascertain and comprehend all Truth. It is in this way that wisdom comes to justify her children and define the men that are of good value to be sages for all ages.

The ingredient of the fulfilling, enduring and sustainable is encapsulated in the son who proves to be worthy before

Heaven. He is a faithful custodian entrusted by the Divine to be the courier of the precious things needed for regeneration. All the sons dwell in the palm of the heavenly Father as stars to be used as the foundation of the new heaven on earth. The sons will not deny or refuse whoever comes to ask of them in sincere belief and true confession. Many will be led to them in spirit for destiny always leads the earmarked on to the path of redemption. To be earmarked is to be favored through grace and it is marvelous to behold. The sons do not speak by themselves or for themselves but are rather earthly voices who relay Truth whispered into their hearts to others. They point out the way for humanity to follow and spot obstacles to avoid. In so doing, they impart due knowledge and wisdom to the ignorant so that the unwary can become aware of the dangers that lurk ahead. Those who are attentive to them have a good chance to reach the golden shores of eternity but those who do not have little.

Many in the world are spiritually sick, blind and trapped in hopelessness. The battle that dogs mankind's earthly existence, both individually and collectively, is in the spirit. The state of his spirit is manifested and can be ascertained in mankind's external surroundings. The unbelieving and faithless man fights a losing battle for he uses the wrong tools of the flesh to fight ravages visited on him in the spirit. The sons do not fight with the power and might of the flesh but in the spirit of the living God who is the final arbiter of the things that matter in life. All who heed the plea of wisdom to change ways and reconnect with the Divine will have outstanding changes take place in their lives. All who have been changed for better and proven in the fire of Truth must walk in charity and live in sacrificial love. Such must live as curators of the unchanging and enduring who live to give and receive from the spirit of the everlasting.

The lust of the flesh and earthly possessions becloud spiritual sight and debase mankind's spirit. The debased or base man is not able to perceive the spiritual for that within him is dead. The sons of God travel along on their earthly walk anonymously. They are obscured to the base man but ablaze in starry brilliance to the seeker of Truth. The true seeker need only put his faith in God and trust the word of Truth. He will be led in spirit to the source of living water for God always makes room for one more. New life will spring up in and around where there is sincere belief. But the seeker must be willing to let go of all that he has ever known for a new vista to be opened to him. Life within the divine fold is a strange new way but it holds the promise of peace, fulfillment and victory in life.

The seeker that walks after Christ must be willing to allow the Divine to take over total control and leadership of his life. He must yield as tugged in the heart and follow along as led in spirit. It is a total commitment that he must keep through all the seasons of life for he has entered into a spiritual union. It is a marriage of the willing and purified in Truth which can never be broken. The faithful believer lives continuously in Christ even as the latter lives in him. The heart of the seeker who has become bonded with Christ is much sought after and loved by the heavenly Father. Such a chosen heart will belong with God forever for he has become a son in same order as Christ Jesus.

The yoke of Christ is easy but the trail is narrow. The way of the world appears to be easy and free-willing but it leads to a dead end. Mankind should be wary for the world is a lie that masquerades as the true. Wisdom cautions all to be wary of the world's promises. Its way is to sugarcoat everything so as to mislead the blind to equate goodness with the easy and sweet. The good things in life start off difficult and challenging but end up sweet. The good things are built up on a foundation of Truth with good purpose. The good thing is taxing but pays back handsomely in the end. The good thing is borne of wisdom in the light of truth. But the ware of the world is too expensive, rewards little and wears down man's soul to nothing over time.

- ✓ The believer that is fully matured in Christ has not become perfect but has met a certain threshold.
- ✓ The sons are endued with prescient knowledge so as to be well-informed about issues that matter.
- ✓ The faithful who forgives in mercy will have the memory and guilt of his past sins surely fade away.
- ✓ The constant refrain and song of hope of the faithful should be redeeming love on to salvation.
- ✓ The sons dwell in the palm of the heavenly Father as foundation for the new heaven on earth.
- ✓ The faithless fights a losing battle when he uses the flesh to fight the ravages visited on him in spirit.
- ✓ The sons walk in anonymity on earth obscured to the faithless but ablaze in spirit to seekers.
- ✓ The heart chosen by God as a dwelling place belong in the divine fold forever as one christened in light.
- ✓ The mind of Christ can give cause to all such that brings fullness and fulfillment in life.
- ✓ The ware of the world is too expensive, rewards little and gradually wears down man's soul.

Certainty makes for simplicity and orderliness

But variance does breed complications in life

Heaven's blessings alight not on the uncertain

Neither will hope attend in strife or confusion

Chapter 13

PEACE FOR THE CERTAIN

The believer who is spiritually reconciled with God will subsequently be at peace within and with all things in creation. He will begin to hear the inaudible whispers that come from all that surrounds him. The ear of the spirit within him will be tuned to pick up much of what everything around him is communicating. He will realize that he has become a wireless receiver that walks about in a sea of information that most men are not aware of. Because he is spiritually in tune with the Creator and creation, he is given to walk on the path of righteousness for only those who are can do so. As a result, he will no longer cast about blindly wherever, whenever and however in life for he can see in true light to be sure of where he is going. He will in effect begin to live a focused and purposed life suited to produce outcomes that delight the heart as well as please the heavenly Father.

He who walks on the path of righteousness will cease from cutting corners and looking for short cuts in his earthly endeavors. He will come to fully understand that there is a right way and appointed seasons to do things. He will catch the spirit that leads mankind to make the path straight, lay the foundation square and build things the right way. Such is the spirit that attends full maturity in Christ and embodies the divine wind of change that heralds the everlasting. Full maturity in the spirit of Christ is the issuing forth of God's blessed anointing and the projection of divine light on the faithful seeker. The wind of change that heralds full maturity in Christ is often a stormy whirlwind that sweeps away the old to reset things in new light for the seeker. The stormy wind is the hammerhead for breaking up the hard and stony ground so that it may be won over for God. The soil is prepared well before Christ arrives to plant the divine precious seeds, the candle stand is positioned before the candle is lit and the lesser is laid out before the greater is tendered.

It is of no use to learn all the words of scripture but miss the spirit of new life in Christ embodied within the words. He who knows and can quote all of scripture but lacks the divine anointing of the spirit within those words has nothing. He will never be able to fulfill the spirit of the law though he may quote and spout them. He who has the spirit of Truth may not know all that is written about God's laws but he will be divinely guided to fulfill them. There is an underlying truth and a common thread that runs through the scriptures that is difficult for many to 'see'. It is difficult because they lack the faith to trust God who they cannot see. They lack the wisdom and spiritual guidance to fathom words that are often divinely cloaked in the purest of light. The words of scriptures are really about the Spirit of God presenting the same Truth in 'diverse manners and sundry times' to mankind that is hard of hearing in the hope that it will get through at the appointed time for him to comprehend in better light.

The heavenly Father will bend down and do all he can to meet man at his lowly intransigent level. He who knows a little scripture and lives by that is far better than he who knows a lot but will not live by what he knows. The former is a faithful believer but the latter is a noisy drum that is filled with empty words. His words though plentiful and enthralling will lack the power of divine anointing. He that is filled with such empty words has fallen into the sin of the scribes and Pharisees. The door that leads to the Father eludes such but yet they refuse to allow those that know to show the way. The believer who writes the words of scripture in the tablet of his heart and lives accordingly will be instructed into the hidden truths and mysteries. He will lay up a priceless treasure in his heart from which will spring forth things that are new but old. He will duly become privy to the unspoken things of God understood only as the Holy Ghost speaks to the faithful heart.

The scriptures cease to be just words when the faithful

become privy to the hidden truths. Only then do the words coalesce into pictures which show up repeatedly all over. Colors and shades within the pictures may differ but the contents remain the same. It is God using certain people in certain ways to highlight and contrast the two ways of life on earth. One is the way of Christ which leads to life and the other is the way of the world that leads to death. The characters may differ but the underlying truth and outcome remain the same. The encompassing message is that man does not stand a chance against evil by himself. He needs divine intervention to help him and he can have it through Christ. Christ Jesus is the way of escape that God has set aside so mankind can overcome the prince of the darkness of this world. He that trusts in the faithful promise that God has made through Christ will grow in spirit to 'see' the pictures in the scriptures. As he lives in faithful obedience to that seen, he will grow from glimpsing the pictures to fully comprehend the harmony and timeless treasure within the whole of God's truth.

The faithful that gets the picture and understands the harmony within the scriptures has become an eater of the fruit of the fig tree. The words of scripture are mostly figurative but yet true and fulfilling. This is the mystery and the genius of God's divine mind. The fig tree is the tree of life whose fruit can only be afforded by those who have attained a certain level of spiritual maturity. He who eats and digests the fruit of the fig tree will be in communion with the Divine. God communicates in pictures for it is a universal medium that needs no translation. It is indeed true that one picture is better than a thousand words. It is also true that one who is in communal fellowship with God can chase a thousand that are faithless. Language is a local medium that divides and separates mankind. It muddles and limits communion of spirit among humanity. It was instituted at Babel in order to throw man for a loop. It is a way for the heavenly Father to instruct mankind that there are such things that cannot be accomplished by human strength or power but in the spirit of the living God. It is a way for God to let mankind know that he only determines who is spiritually worthy regardless of what each man thinks of self. It is a preventive measure to preclude mankind from taking the base things of the earth to Heaven. It is God's way to tell all that mankind must first be purified in spirit by living in obedience to the words of Truth before he can afford to ascend to the starry heights to then bring the heavenly down to earth.

The faithful believer who can ascend to the heavenly heights is able to see the true picture of the world that God sees. He will no longer be deceived by the worldly for his eyes can 'see' from the mountain top. He has ascended to the summit of the mount where mankind is transfigured and soaked in the pure mist of true understanding. The transfigured is a living tabernacle not planted in one place but able to go in spirit as the Father sends him. Such is given to communicate less with words but more in pictures and actions. The medium of pictures is the language of light and truth. A picture leaves a true impression on the mind that tells no lies. It is the most faithful and effective medium to teach the mind, feed the soul and nourish man's spirit. The words of scripture paint one grand picture of his glorious family as God instructs mankind about outcomes, fruits, works and end results. God speaks not about persons but about his family. There comes a season in the life of every faithful believer when he begins to see himself and his place within that family. When that comes about, he will become the selfless in spirit who has entered the season of restoration where goodness and mercy readily come to attend him in life.

Simply put, restoration is the process of bringing things back to how they should be or putting contents back into the empty. It is the means by which things are re-created or new things are brought out from the old. Restoration emanates from the hub of creation which is at the heart of God. It is from thence that the power to rebuild broken down things and to bring dead things back to life issue forth. There is usually a set of problems that appear mountainous and insurmountable to the believer at the commencement of restoration. It takes divine wisdom bestowed from the heavenly Father to afford the believer the means to break down the mountainous that confronts him. Only then will he discover that within the mountain in the way are the seeds that God will use to glorify him.

The seeds of glory are already there but are found as gold dust sprinkled in the stream of living water that flows within the mountain in the way. The seeds of glory are found within that which had seemed to block the way. But first the seeker must be shown the way into the heart of the mountain. A way has to be made for him where hitherto none had seemed to be. A cleft has to be made for him in the Rock. The eye of the inner man has to be opened so that he can see that which has always been there but not perceived. The seeker could not see before because his spirit had been cast down by the heavy cross that he had to carry. He did not realize then that the burden of the cross will free the spirit within him to see in greater light. Only the free in spirit can afford the coin that is the toll to Providence. The coin affords the donkey that the seeker rides in his 'Hosanna' parade so he can enter into the peace that passes understanding. The donkey is that vehicle which has been prepositioned and tethered for the seeker. The vehicle is there but it can only be seen in the true and pure humble light of Christ. It is the vehicle by which the faithful come into Providence and under the mercy of God. And so by divine mercy the faithful in Christ come to be justified and shown a way out of troubles.

The process of restoration begins with full immersion in Truth but concludes with baptism in the fire of the spirit of

Christ. Immersion in Truth or the baptism of John serves to keep the spiritual walk of the believer simple, orderly and purposed. Simplicity, orderliness and purpose lead to certainty. Complexity, disorderliness and variance lead to uncertainty. God does not restore the uncertain or bless the confused. The shell of the mountain in the way of restoration protects the valuable seeds hidden within its heart. The seeds are capsules of the glorious that have been touched by the hand of the Divine and watered by the purified mists of Truth. Once planted, the seeds of glory will sprout to kiss the heavens and branch out to touch the horizons so that all men can see what the hand of the Lord has done. And so the mountain that confronts the faithful in the way always breaks out in joyful song to induce mankind to praise God for his marvelous doings.

The faithful believer that has been entrusted with seeds of the glorious must be diligent to plant them for such are precious. The seeds of glory are framed in great vision. Great vision takes strong faith to be made manifest so all can see what God has done. The trustee of the seed must put the 'spirit' of discouragement behind so that he can embrace the spirit of power and a sound mind. This can only happen when he connects to the Holy Spirit through Christ. The Holy Spirit is the enabler of the faithful. The heavenly Father will not deny the request of the trustee of his priceless seeds. He who carries the priceless seeds is God's chosen vessel to be used for glory. God hides the seeds of glory in hearts where the enemy cannot touch such. Every trustee of the seed is also shielded from the corruption of worldliness so that he can remain prepared to be the good steward in the season of restoration.

God confides in the chosen in order to avail knowledge that is hidden from others. In this season of information overload, true wealth is knowledge that is not commonly available. Knowledge and wisdom from the divine Father is given freely but it is not free. It is not to be misused or abused but used for glorious service in God's name through Christ. The fullness of the riches in the divine treasure chest is limitless. The custodian of the priceless must remove himself from doubters and anything else that will distract him from the purpose ordained for him. He must plant so that he can have abundant harvest as due. Abundance is his due reward for faithfulness and love for God. Such is the harvest that awaits the good custodian who faithfully plants as God instructs and the spirit leads.

The faithful believer that has come into restoration has intermeddled with and been grafted into the source of all wisdom. He must remain there with Christ at the center of his life so that he can continue in victorious living. He must continue to walk in the light of Christ so as to be assured of abundant harvest for his labors. He must the divine command that all pass through the door of Christ always in order to find both spiritual and earthly nourishment. The blood of the Lamb of sacrifice must be on the doorposts of his heart to serve and protect him in his going out and coming in. He that is in restoration has died and is resurrected with Christ. He has become the selfless with a new name and new life that no longer lives for self but for all. It is for such in restoration that God has promised never to leave or forsake. This is victory promised, victory hoped for and victory attained. It is life triumphant realized through Christ. The custodian of the precious seed must not seek after the praise of men for such praise perverts the gift and infects the seed. He must remain in the wings and let God take center stage so as to remain justified in all his ways. He must protect the divine seeds in the treasure chest of his heart with diligent love so that he may continue to bring out things that are new but old.

The believer can only protect the precious by immersion and obedience to Truth in the light of Christ. Obedience to truth offers the believer a chance to clean up his spiritual life. It affords the faithful a means to shake off the world and have a chance to be sprinkled with the dust of eternity. Truth eliminates areas of spiritual weakness in the life of the believer that may expose him to attack and possible defeat by the forces of darkness. Immersion in Truth is the rinsing off of the residual mud cake of the world so that the faithful can be primed for the eternal. It is the final preparation before the faithful believer who has been seeking after him can finally meet up with Christ.

Immersion in Truth serves to disengage the halting and hindering in the life of the seeker so that he can never be left behind again once he has met up with Christ. Immersion in Truth or baptism of John can be likened to Moses leading the Hebrews of old to the doorsteps of the new land wherein he cannot enter. It is the transition from the highest of the less into the lowest of the greater. It is being called up from the minor to the major league of faith. Baptism in Truth changes and resets the perspective of the believer permanently from the earthly to the heavenly. It helps him to keep his eyes fixed and his heart tuned to God. It serves to remind the seeker why he is here, what he should be doing with his time, how he should be doing it and who he should be doing it for. Full immersion or baptism in Truth is the last cleansing of the mind before the faithful is ushered into the order of Christ.

The faithful believer that has met up to be ushered into the order of Christ will seem to be alone but he is not for he has entered into a select company. He is connected in spirit to an unseen innumerable host with Christ Jesus leading the way. There will be times when he may appear to be that lone voice in a wilderness filled with the deaf and blind determined to go their own way but going nowhere really. It is in such times that he may weary, worry and wonder if he has labored in vain and for naught. But he must persevere in nurturing the seed of Truth entrusted to him for such never fails to bear fruit in due season. God's work may be stymied for a while but it is never stopped as long as it is accompanied by strong faith and great vision.

There is a cycle of the feeling of emptiness followed by that of revival that accompanies work in the kingdom of God. And so the laborer for God needs to be spiritually refilled in between so that he may in turn fill others in a repetitive cycle. It is like recharging a battery depleted after usage for the next duty cycle. It is the vessel being empowered by the Master to be used for works of glory. The believer not used in this stead will have nothing to show for his faith for the validation and utility value of the vessel lies in its usage to do work pleasing to God. The chosen may appear little in the eyes of the world and be marginalized to the fringes of society yet he occupies an exalted place in the universal scheme of things. He will grow from the 'little one' to stand up in the congregation of the mighty before God and bask in the glory of faithful service to the Divine.

- ✓ It takes reconciliation with God for man to find peace within and with all things in creation.
- ✓ He that quotes the words of scripture but lacks the spirit therein in him has nothing before God.
- ✓ The underlying reason for God's gift of Christ is that man does not stand a chance against evil alone.
- ✓ The mystery of God's sacred truths is that such are figurative yet true and ever fulfilled.
- ✓ The fully matured in spirit can ascend to the exalted realm to perceive the world as God does.
- ✓ The seeds of glory lie within faith-mountain as sprinkles of golden dust in a stream of living water.
- ✓ Only God can avail mankind the seed of glory that sprouts from earth to heaven when planted.
- ✓ God hides the seed of glory in the heart of the faithful believer where the enemy cannot touch it.
- ✓ Obedience to Truth removes the hindering so the seeker never falls behind once joined with Christ.
- ✓ The works of glory may be stymied for a while by the enemy but such are never stopped.

Humanity's true face can be seen in love

Where the enduring and fulfilling abound

In a place where meekness rules the heart

And in a time to seek redress not impress

Chapter 14

LIGHT IN A DARK SEA

The heavenly heights offer a unique perspective from which to view life on earth in a true and pure light. Seen from above, the earth is a sea of darkness interspersed with points of light. The points of light are those whose souls have been washed by the words of Truth and whose hearts have been lit as altars to serve God and humanity in love. The darkness that surrounds the points of light is the pervasive evil found within the hearts of many in the world. However God's eyes are forever fixed on the points of light in doting love to protect them from the evil wind of the worldly that surrounds them.

Every heart lit with the flame of love is so much treasured by God that his ear is always ready to hear their prayers. It is on account of such high regard for them, which must not be overlooked, that God is very much concerned with protecting them from the darkness and evil that surrounds them in the world. It is for such whose hearts have been lit as candles that the bowls of goodness and tender mercies are laid out. Heaven's offerings to mankind can be thought of as bowls filled with life's good gifts as well as acts of goodness and mercy tendered in love. The contents of the bowls are there to delight the hearts lit aflame with love as it pleases the heavenly Father for they are joined with him in spirit through Christ. Such hearts are tabernacles for the spirit of God to dwell and also vessels through which mercy is poured out on earth.

Every heart aflame with love has been prepared to serve as a vessel of mercy on earth with the light of Christ as life's guide. Such vessels often suffer much adversity in the world for love of God and devotion to Christ. Yet they remain willingly to endure and persevere after Christ to the end. Rejection and undeserved hatred by the world on account of love for God and Truth never deter the truly faithful. They refuse to cast blame but choose rather to ask for God's forgiveness for the ignorance of men. The willingness to bear the shame and loneliness of the cross in grace serves to validate the faithful before God. Such grace commends the faithful in Christ well to make communion between the heavenly and earthly possible. He that can commune in that light has become a hybrid of two worlds that can go for other men where they are not able to go. He can listen in on things that other men are not able to hear and share knowledge garnered thereby. In effect, he has joined in the divinely ordained mission to bring wisdom from heavenly to earthly places in the light of Christ to help remake earth in the order of Heaven.

The curse of Babel is reversed for him that has been divinely appointed to help remake earth in the order of Heaven. He will be divinely availed the universal language of Truth whereby all in creation will understand him and he will understand them in spirit. The wall of division that separates mankind will be broken down for him so that he will come to dwell in spirit where all feed together in peace. He will be given to speak in figures and frame pictures with words. The pictures that he frames with his words have been glimpsed with the eye of the inner man. Such pictures reflect Truth by which God's divine will is manifested. God's will is forward looking and leads to the future. The ultimate will of God is regeneration for his creation. He that is privy to divine will is also availed the means to revitalize necessary things in life. He will be led in spirit to do the right thing at the right time as one who has come into the season of regeneration. However such must proceed with due diligence and use that availed to get God's business duly done with his time on earth.

It costs the believer his place in the world and many of the wanted things in life before he can come into the season of regeneration. The latter is found under mercy by those that wisely sought after the kingdom of God first. He that has come into the season of regeneration has a confidence which pervades his nature and governs everything that he says and does. It is this other-worldly confidence that communicates that Christ has come to full maturity within the believer and that which attracts many to Truth.

The gift of Christ fully matured and arisen in the believer must be used to serve humanity and bring God due glory. The matured in Christ must be ready at all times to bear testimony to others about the confidence that frames his life. It is confidence borne of unrequited love, unbreakable promises and the blessings of the heavenly Father which has come to attend his life. The spirit of fear departs to be replaced by that of power and a sharp mind when Christ matures and is arisen within the believer. He that is bestowed with such power and a sharp mind must remain faithful always to serve God's will in true light.

Christ knows what the future will look like for mankind. He knows what will be needful in the future and what will not be. It all works together under God's provident will to yield the enduring and fulfilling for the faithful believer. It is life divinely appointed in the light of Christ for those that dwell under the mercy of God. In order to be worthy to be called therein, the believer must remain a clean vessel, holy and acceptable to be used by God. Surely the earth is his creation but the heavenly Father needs the faithful who understand his way to help manage things the right way.

There is a mass of men and women all over the world that

love and follow in light after Christ to God's approval. They have followed in good faith to meet up with Christ in that place close to the heart of God. Such are perfect before God as mankind can be but continuously garnering the attributes of the divine in an unending everlasting process. They are the beloved of God held in the protective palm of his hand as one carefully holds the precious pearl. The stars of the night sky are emblematic of them. Each star occupies the place ordained for it from the beginning of time to help spell out God's plan and intention for the perceptive eye to see. In the same wise, the faithful are led to occupy the earthly lots that the Father has ordained for them as starry spirits to shine thereabouts in reflection of his divine will. In the fullness of time, as they complete their earthly round, these starry spirits do return to their heavenly abode as the chosen given to twinkle in love and life everlasting within the Divine fold.

God's plan and intentions are there for the perceptive in spirit to see in the night sky. The writings in the night sky can only be read by the chosen that have been bestowed with the eye to do so. The latter are the matured in Christ that are privy to the divine will. Such have passed judgment in God's eye so that nothing is hidden from them. The writings spell out divine edicts that are there for everyone to see for the sky is a universal canvas. Sadly most men are spiritually blind and not aware that the writings are there. Others are sight impaired and know that the writings are there but are unable to read them. However a select few can see and read them. These are the bearers of his divine light who have been chosen for eternal life with the heavenly Father. Such pass through the world and leave a trail of enlightenment everywhere during their brief sojourn on earth. They leave handiworks that shine before men and are showcases for God's endowments on mankind to be fully displayed. Those who follow them will never go wrong for they are vehicles used to carry out the divine sovereign will on earth.

The matured in Christ have been nurtured in the cocoon of love under divine mercy as the seedlings of the unfolding re-creation of the earth. They are the embryos that will be transplanted to populate the new that looms on the horizon. These worthy souls are the link between the passing world and the emerging one. As the current age passes away because it is appointed for all earthly things to die, another will emerge as the new Heaven on earth. The faithful and worthy before God comprise the nursery for the new earth to come. They are enmeshed in a perfecting process within the cocoon of God's love to be transformed therein into the divine image. Such are then used to induce those that interact with them on earth into a spiritual awakening in the light of Christ.

The whole of creation is waiting for noble in spirit bred in the cocoon of love under mercy and changed into a divine image to show in full force. Their experience in the cocoon of love translates into the pattern for victorious living that will be manifested in the new age of the earth to come. Their time and experience in the cocoon of God's love has prepared them in spirit with the knowledge needed to master the future. And so, they have become the visionaries and guiding lights appointed to lead mankind into a better future. Without consciously being aware of it, such are living at the present time as mankind will come to live in the future that awaits humanity. As this age comes to its inevitable end, there will be a cosmic silence or turning around point when things will change to trend upwards to the good and perfect.

The season of the good and perfect is that which creation is waiting for. It is the season that heralds the glorious dawn of humanity. It is the dawn of the day of the new man in Christ purified of heart and noble in spirit. It is the age for those who have chosen the fruit of the tree of life through Christ. Such have chosen the wisdom of God over the fruit of the knowledge of good and evil which stokes the darkness in the world. All who choose wisdom will no longer settle for less and exhaust precious time to seek an impossible balance between good and evil. Rather they will break free from evil to finally attain the good and perfect which has always been the heavenly Father's wish for mankind from the beginning of creation. All who are appointed to see the dawn of the good and perfect are duly woven into the fabric of life. All who are woven therein have realized the everlasting from which there is no separation for it is death swallowed up in victory by life.

All who have been chosen for the new age are also bestowed with a life inducing spirit. The things that their embrace will thrive to endure and those things that they reject will not. As couriers of the divine spark in this wise, they embody seeds of new life that bring about a quickening and re-awakening of spirit in the lifeless. That which bring is light that thaws out the wintry in the dormant spirit in order to usher in the spring of new life.

The flesh is the great inhibitor of man's spirit but he needs it for the time of his brief existence on earth. The flesh always wars against the spirit to make man susceptible to the corruption in the world. The ego is the Achilles heel of man in the warfare between his spirit and flesh. Man's ego is really nothing but a misconceived notion of his self-importance. If the truth is to be told, mankind flesh is of little consequence in the overall scheme of things. He is barely here today and gone tomorrow so to speak. The redeemable entity in mankind is his spirit if such can be duly awakened and transformed into new life in Christ.

- ✓ The exalted realm offers a unique perspective from which to view life on earth in a pure and true light.
- ✓ The willingness to bear the shame and loneliness of the cross is that which validates the truly faithful.
- ✓ To be led in spirit to do the right thing at the right time is to re-build in heavenly order.
- ✓ A confident hope pervades and governs the life of the believer that lives in the kingdom of God.
- ✓ The attributes of Godliness are garnered by the faithful in an unending and everlasting process.
- ✓ There is a divine handwriting in the night sky that most men cannot 'see' due to spiritual blindness.
- ✓ The worthy in faith have been prepared as the nursery for the new age of earth about to unfold.
- ✓ A cosmic silence will happen first before things turn around to point upwards and heavenly.
- ✓ The noble in spirit are woven into the fabric of life to have an inheritance in the good and perfect.
- ✓ The faithful that have been chosen for the new age are bestowed the divine spark that induces life.
- ✓ Man's ego has to be set to naught in order for the spirit of goodness within him to show forth.
- ✓ The ego is the Achilles heel in the warfare between mankind's flesh and the spirit within him.

God's heart is the mansion grand and lovely

The sons are rooms in many hues and colors

Pieces of his heart remade in love and light

As stars of hope to brighten earth's dark veil

Chapter 15

THE SONS WAIT TO SING

The sons of God are being amassed by divine will to be world changers on the grand stage of humanity's affairs. They will be unveiled for all in creation to know and acknowledge only when they reach critical mass. However before the unveiling, the world has to pass through a cleansing that is aimed to sort out things in good order. The world has to pass through a season of disenchantment with illusory grandeur and unbridled consumption so that its taste for the super-sized, glitzy and excessive can subside. It will be like a season of catharsis when a misguided world will be weaned away from the delusion and absurdity of the superfluous. The season of catharsis first has to take place before the unveiling of the sons and the ushering in of the new age of Heaven on earth.

The sons have been spiritually prepared for the works of healing and rebuilding that humanity sorely needs. It is spiritual restoration on a universal scale that evokes the paradise state of Eden. It is restoration of the earth to a new Eden where man, God's favorite creation, can once again walk in fellowship with the heavenly Father. Each son has to know who he has become in Christ before others will come to know him. He has to know before he can learn to use the special services available to him and live up to his true potential. As each son comes to understand the scope of what he can accomplish through the power of God, he must begin the works of restoration for there is little time to waste. Some sons know who they are in Christ but many are yet to fully understand the scope of the power that God has entrusted to them to aid in the healing and restoration of humanity.

The son is that faithful believer who has persevered in faith to grow to full spiritual maturity in Christ. He is the faithful who is communion with the Father and has been availed the gift of the 'comforter'. The 'comforter' is the Holy Ghost and is given so that the recipient can be privy to the heavenly Father's will. He that has received the 'comforter' lives under divine mercy so that he will come to do all things in the spirit of the living God. Such is one who has been measured, found worthy and divinely fitted to be used for works that bring God glory on earth.

The faithful believer who has been fitted for this divine service by God is a vessel calibrated with Christ as the standard of reference. He is able to receive the new wine availed to the faithful through Christ. Such has received a place in God's kingdom as one given to model the way whereby mankind can realize the divine. He will have the right words at the right time for every situation for he is not the one that speaks when he does but the Spirit that dwells within him. In effect, he will become a ruler of men in that whatever he says or does will come to be the order of the day. He is one who no longer strives by his might but given to do the amazing in the Spirit of the living God.

He that has the spirit of life dwelling within to speak through him wields a powerful sword in the service of God. He has to master how to wield the sword through humility and faithful obedience in order to remain victorious over the prince of the darkness of this world. This mastery is crucial as each son embarks on re-creating the earthly in heavenly order. But first the source of the darkness of the world has to be subjugated by divine power acting through the sons before lasting change can come about. Only then can the groundswell to re-create the earth in heavenly order take full effect and lead to the great dawn of humanity. The earth and mankind is God's prized creation but the prince of the darkness of this world has made a mockery of it with his seductive but false ways. He has led humanity away from the way of love down to the path of futility, dissatisfaction, emptiness, diseases, simmering conflicts, hatred, wars and hopelessness. But his time is fast running out as there is an emerging and trending consensus within the hearts of many that there has to be a better way. Deep down in the heart, mankind knows that God did not intend for him to live the way he does and for the earth to be abused the way it is.

The sons of God are bestowed with the mind of Christ so that their will is joined individually and collectively with that of the heavenly Father. The mind of Christ affords the ability to be a good custodian of God's creation. Before his fall, Adam knew what the plants and animals were created for. He understood their purposes and therefore called them by their proper names for his mind was in harmony with that of God. It is that same ability that each son possesses. Each has an innate and instinctive ability to understand what creation and everything within it is designated for. The whole of creation is God's mansion. The sons live in their father's mansion and know what each room and contents are for. They have glimpsed the pattern of things in Heaven and are led by the Spirit of God to 'project' the same on earth. This project of restoration is on-going all over the world as led by the Spirit of God and under a timeline well managed by Divine will.

The sons are called to enlarge their tabernacles so that the seed for the new Heaven on earth can be propagated by their individual and collective actions. By such efforts others will observe their initiatives and subconsciously copy them. It is the will and power of God that acts through those that are called to fulfill diverse divine purposes on earth among mankind. The sons have been predestinated and positioned all over the world in accordance with God's grand plan. No portion of humanity or corner of the earth has been left out so that God will always remain blameless. The sons of light are to be found among all cultures, colors, countries and tongues. The darker the corner of the earth is the purer and more blazing the light within the son positioned there. All the sons embody the universal brotherhood of the living church of Christ and constitute the new Israel.

Each son is connected in spirit to God as an outlet of the divine impetus on earth and as a conduit for those things which flow down from the heavenly throne. In a certain sense the sons can be likened to personal computers that are connected with God the Supercomputer. All due knowledge requisite for the moment is passed on to them from the all-knowing Supercomputer as needed. It is in this context that the Holy Spirit can be likened to the electrical power that energizes the network of computers while the Holy Ghost conveys the information that courses through the network. It is in this way that the sons have cast up the highway to God for their minds are linked up in an information grid through which the wisdom and will of God courses down to earth. But each son must remain sanctified in Truth in order to remain true to that which flows from the throne of God above and reject the false that corrupts borne of the earthy from below.

Truth is the transformer that conditions the power of God to make it effective for doing all kinds of good work. It takes Truth to nullify the attempts of the enemy to stop the spiritual growth and earthly endeavors of the seeker after Christ. Truth prevents and minimizes the damage that the prince of the darkness of this world can inflict on the believer. The believer that has embraced Truth to let it govern his earthly affairs already lives in Godliness. Such a believer who lives his life in the spirit of Truth will always find God to be at hand for him. Truth is also the firewall that shields the knowledge and wisdom entrusted to the faithful from corruption by the enemy. It is the membrane that ideally shields the message of Christ in transmission, conveyance and reception so as to remain pure. It takes Truth to nourish body, mind and spirit in light for it is the essence of the divine and only means to keep evil at bay.

The sons who are connected in spirit to the mind of God are given to understand the mysteries and the sacred hidden truths. They are given access to knowledge precluded from those that deny Truth and the hypocrites that compromise it. It is information communicated to the sons in this light that enables them to be the standard bearers for God that others follow in the light of Christ. And so such live and work to make that which has been conceived in the mind of God to be actualized on earth.

All the sons embody the spirit of regeneration that brings

and sustains new life in the light of Christ. They share and communicate due knowledge within this assembly of renewal through Christ life in truth and love. The assembly is God's mercy program where the chosen are prepared as seedlings for re-creating the earth in new order. Each believer that is part of this assembly may be likened to a nymph that will emerge with God's other sons in due season fitted and entrusted with the knowledge as well as wisdom to 'rule' the earth in heavenly order.

There is always a delay and hesitation before the commitment to answer God's call from when it is first heard. However he who has been divinely earmarked will eventually respond to the call. The response may be gradual because the inertia of worldliness resists change and takes time to be overcome. It takes about three years to build up a commitment to trust God. To let go of the worldly is the spiritual beast that the believer has to wrestle with and overcome before he can stand with Christ. The battle for man's soul is fought between the old life which the believer has known and the new which he is yet to know. Unless God has earmarked him for victory in this fight, the chance for mankind to prevail in this struggle of the old versus new is very slim.

The believer that has won the battle of the old versus the new will thereafter be in the world but no longer belong to it. He will embark on a search guided by the inaudible voice of the Spirit of God to ascertain the Truth as well as power in the words of scripture. Only then has he truly begun to follow in the footsteps of Christ with a good chance of meeting up with him in due time. It takes at least fourteen more years of devoted commitment to mature in the way to meet up with Christ and be ushered into the kingdom of God. There are several ways to aptly describe this spiritual state when the faithful has met up with Christ. It can be said that he has found the room reserved for him in God's mansion or that his soul has become anchored on the solid rock of God. There are numerous other ways of declaring it but the truth is that he has met up with Christ to become reconciled and reconnected with God in spirit.

The believer that has reconnected with God in spirit is much like a lost traveler who has found his way back home by listening for the pulse of Christ. There is a homing device that God has placed in man to serve as a directional finder when needed. This is what it means to be foreknown and pre-destined. But the directional finder can only be powered by Truth and receives only the pulse of Christ. The latter is food to enlighten the soul and revive the dead spirit so the lost can find the way home to God.

- ✓ God has positioned his sons over the world as he works out his plans to give humanity a new start.
- ✓ The sons have been prepared for the healing and restoration of humanity on a universal scale.
- ✓ The faithful that lives by Truth written in his heart will be divinely guided in his endeavors.
- ✓ The faithful fitted for noble service is calibrated with Christ as the standard of reference.
- ✓ The spirit of darkness has to be subjugated through Christ for healing and restoration to take hold.
- ✓ The sons of light have an innate and instinctive understanding of what creation should be like.
- ✓ The sons have been prepositioned by the Divine among all cultures, colors, countries and tongues.
- ✓ Each son of God is a conduit for things which flow from the heavenly throne to reach mankind below.
- ✓ The sons live and work to make that conceived in the mind of God to be actualized on earth.
- ✓ The sons of God are part of the universal web of regeneration that brings and sustains new life.
- ✓ The truly faithful in Christ are guided in spirit to ascertain the Truth and power in God's words.
- ✓ The heart of the faithful believer is linked up with the Divine in love through Truth.

From the starry realm man looks ahead

To the place of good hope and renewal

For backwards leads to a misguided past

To recrimination and accusations galore

Chapter 16

IN THE WILDERNESS

The believer that has fully matured in Christ lives on a spiritual housetop as one given to take the high road in life. It is from there that man's spiritual eye can remain fixed on God as he goes about his calling. He that dwells thereon will be at peace within. He will also have an innumerable company of spiritual messengers at his behest to help him accomplish all that God has assigned for him to do on earth. No one has seen God but the fully matured in Christ are the closest that mankind can come to learn about his nature for they are bestowed with many of his attributes. When mankind begins to seek and call on God sincerely, he will be invariably drawn to one who is matured in spirit to observe and learn from. Any seeker that has one matured in Christ revealed to him must open his heart to receive the gift of enlightenment in love. All who are matured in Christ are God's elect to offer up sacrifices and receive spiritual gifts on behalf of others in love. However such gifts are given freely but there are not free for the faith of the recipient will be sorely tested.

One of the favorite tactics of the enemy of Truth is to put a cloak over the eye of the young believer. He does so by attempting to take him back to the past. The way of Christ offers a new life separate from the past. The two cannot be mixed together but the enemy of God is a master at repackaging the old to look like the new. He cleverly repackages the old in order to beguile and mislead the unwary back to the past that should be left behind. The young believer is a favorite target of the ploys of the enemy aimed at deceiving the young in faith. Quite often the latter are not yet fully established in Christ, may be partaking of God's grace unworthily or struggling to let go of the ungodly ways of the past. A quite effective tactic of the enemy is to falsely accuse the matured in Christ as a blundering heretic with strange ideas so that the young believer may not embrace true light.

The enemy often poses as an angel of light but the Truth is that he works to shield out true light with offerings that turn out to be good for nothing in the end. The enemy is a hypocrite who is never humble or show contrition before God for that is his nature. For that reason, he has been denied the true and fulfilling by God. And so, he works to hinder mankind from receiving same. Humility and true contrition matters a lot with God. The prideful is without contrition in spirit and has unwittingly made room for the enemy in his life. Pride hinders mankind from the fellowship of true light availed through Christ. Fellowship within this elect spiritual company is to be desired by all that seek after Christ for therein true knowledge and divine wisdom abound to be received in love.

The cloak that the prince of darkness attempts to throw over the eye of the believer is usually derived from the traditions and ceremony of the old ways. The old ways becloud the eye of the spirit and impede the intrusion of true light into the heart. It takes total commitment to Christ and a disconnection from the old ways to come into the fellowship of true light. The old has to die before the believer can be transformed in the new light of Christ in divine likeness. The old way funnels mankind into a spiritual coffin but the new way through Christ opens up a new life of endless possibilities.

There should be no room for double mindedness when mankind has chosen the way of Christ. One cannot look backwards and forwards at the same time as he follows after Christ. He will become stagnated in his faith life and not be able to meet up with Christ duly if he does so. This is what many that profess to follow after Christ do when they are beguiled into mixing the old with new. In so doing, they play right into the hands of the enemy. The enemy of true light beguiles the unwary into double-mindedness and uncertainty of faith. First the believer must make the disconnection from the old ways so that he can be able to meet up with Christ. After he has met up with Christ or become spiritually transformed, he will be well prepared to change the old way in the better light of the new. Such is to seek the kingdom of God first before other things and it is the blessed way. Such is wisdom that avails a way of escape from the shackles of the old so that one can afford the new and better in divine light.

The believer that has escaped the old and met up with Christ will be bestowed with the mind of the Master for whom he has left all to seek after. The believer who has met up with Christ has not only grown to full spiritual maturity but has become a son of God as well. He has become prepared in spirit to accomplish such great and marvelous works ordained to bring due God glory. He has become an agent to extend mankind's vision of God so that others can experience divine light and power. God searches very hard to find those worthy of the call of Christ. Many that answer the call prove not to be worthy. Only a few prove to be worthy for many cannot bear the shame and burden of the cross. Those who prove worthy are those that become duly christened as sons of God. There is great joy in Heaven on account of those found worthy of the calling of Christ so that a host of heavenly messengers is at their behest to aid them in all endeavors. With such aid, they are given to go beyond the gates of the known and outside the box of human understanding to where others cannot go. They can go to that place hitherto unknown where a new vista awaits to unfold.

The heart that hears and heeds the call of God must be willing to persevere through many challenges. He will be led away by the spirit of the call from all that he has known in the past into a place previously unknown to him. But he must remain committed to Christ so as to be tuned to God and realize the full promises of his new-found land. The spirit of God does not shout as that of the world does. He speaks in a still small voice that is best heard in quiet solitude. And so, the believer is often led away into the wilderness to begin the transformation that leads him to meet up with Christ and into the congregation of the sons. Family, friends and the institutions of his old life will feel let down because he has chosen to put God first in his life above them. But in the fullness of time and with better understanding, many will come to be thankful for the gift of God that he turns out to be for the people.

The faithful in Christ is called not to hold grudges against those that vilify and reject him for many are spiritually ignorant. God saves more of his wrath for those that know but yet sin but less for those that do not know. The faithful that has met up with Christ in the way is asked to deal with all in loving light to share knowledge and wisdom in good faith as needed. He is asked to return to those that lack such to share Truth and wisdom in the light of Christ. It takes such light to highlight the way into the new place where the earthly meets the heavenly. He that has matured in the light of Christ knows that with the passage of time many will come to understand God's way better. They will come to realize that God chooses sons in order to offer them as living sacrifices acceptable for the sins of the people and that many are appointed to embrace Truth through them to find new life. It is by the willingness to suffer on behalf of others that the sons of God demonstrate the nature of divine love.

In the quest to meet up with the divine, many that seek for spiritual fulfillment in the light of Christ do so in the wrong places. They seek in different temples and various places of worship but often fail to find fulfillment thereabouts. This is usually the case when the believer begins to mature in spirit for only the true will fulfill him then. With spiritual maturity, some do come to realize that God is not to be found in a temple of mortar and bricks. Spiritual communion with the Divine does not take place in buildings or groups but in time spent alone seeking to know God better. The time spent in the churches of bricks and mortar serves an introduction to the truth and reality of God. However Christ or the connection to God can only be made by each seeker alone through the heart.

There is a time in spiritual growth when the truly faithful will be called in spirit to venture out into the lonely wilderness so that he can meet up with Christ and thereby come to know the heavenly Father. The true congregation of God is the church without walls and it is found in the lonely wilderness of life by the true seeker. It is much like a mountain located away from the known and familiar that the faithful are called to climb. Often as true seekers are called away from their midst, the churches with walls devolve into congregations of the worldly in spirit where the lust after earthly material assumes primary focus.

And so to mask this truth, the churches with walls often adopt a false posture which equates appearance and material acquisitions as proof of spiritual worthiness before God. But nothing can be further from the truth. The churches with walls or buildings in which people meet in his name do not constitute God's temple. The true temple is the man whose heart God has chosen to be his point of contact with humanity. He is the man whose heart has been washed and whose soul has been purified by Truth. The heart of such a man is the altar of God lit by the flame of love. The man whose heart has been chosen in this light has come into God's confidence. He will be informed of God's will as necessary for he has been led into the commonwealth of the living church of Christ. This congregation embodies the spirits of the justified before God through Christ. The 'heart of God' is the aggregate of such hearts that have been chosen by God as his temple. It is the hub of regeneration where the old becomes new and the dead spring back to new life through Christ.

Each man whose heart is chosen as a temple of the Divine is availed knowledge about significant events to come as due for God will not do anything without letting them know. God is spiritually connected to such that are his temples so that he wills and acts through them as sons to accomplish his divine purposes on earth. To be used in this light is a calling and a way of life ordained for the sons from the foundation of time. It is for this that they were called away from their past lives to be remade in the image of Christ. All remade in that wise must return to offer the new way to their own from whose midst they were called away. Sadly the sons are often not embraced as should but rather rejected. However such rejection never stymies the sons for they will draw others who are 'strangers' to them. Every son that his own rejects will be embraced by others who were not formerly of his own kind for Truth never returns void. In truth God will make sons from any erstwhile sinner willing to embrace light.

Every son is an elect person of destiny who will be known from birth to be a chosen one. All the circumstances and experiences of his life will aggregate to fit the profile of Christ in accordance with the template defined by the words of scriptures. These include questions about his birth circumstances, parentage, heritage, education, struggles, rejection and rebirth in new spirit. Regardless of the tribe, tongue and color the profile is the same. Every son is usually born in the seemingly nondescript house.

This is usually the 'little' house, in the 'little' village but yet he will be of an illustrious linage that can be traced back to the distant past. There is always a sign from the sky when such a one comes into this world and when they depart. Even as children, the elect sons are known to be destined for special missions on earth. However they are often misunderstood while their mission is on-going until the season appointed for it to be understood.

The special mission is a 'new' strange way that had not been known or anticipated by the people. Time always shows the new way to be spiritually uplifting, enlightening, fulfilling and far better than what had been known before. The new is the way of peace and compassion where there is no need for strife. The new way removes the shackles and bondage of the old way so that the willing can be set free to grow in true light to commune with God. The elect sons are universal sprits who travel as emissaries from heavenly to lowly places. They are sent to uplift mankind in spirit so as to realize a better vision of God. They return at the completion of their earthly duties to the heavenly home from whence they are sent down.

Each elect son can be likened to a step in a divine escalator or cosmic wheel that turns from Heaven down to earth and upwards again to rejoin the divine realm. Whoever embraces the way of the elect will be lifted up along with them into the heavenly heights from whence each came down originally. Each elect son has the innate ability to overcome the hold of the world because the inner man of his spirit is conditioned by love of Truth to buoyantly list heavenwards away from the earthen. The sons are the light of the world given as God's gifts to help chase out darkness from humanity's midst. They are used to model the way for those who desire to know God better. Each son is called to share wisdom with those that lack as reasonable service to God and as the means to help them find answers to life's problems in love through light. It is for this reason that they are always and attack by the prince of darkness who seeks to halt the spread of Truth and light. But the sons carry on because they know that the sooner that many embrace Truth is the sooner that the hold of the prince of darkness on the world will be loosed.

Each son of God is a ground breaker called to be a rebuilder of the broken down and a builder of the new in light and love. For this reason he will be under the attack of the prince of darkness. But the attacks of the enemy never deter such that have grown in grace to stand before God under mercy. The attacks do not deter the truly faithful because God is their shield and protection from the enemy. In a paradoxical way, every attack withstood leads to a place closer to the heart of God and to a greater outpouring of divine anointing on the faithful.

- ✓ The matured in spirit dwells on a 'housetop' where his spiritual eyes are always fixed on God.
- ✓ God's gifts are given freely but there are not free for the faith of the receiver will always be tested.
- ✓ The believer must disconnect from the old ways to realize spiritual maturity and divine fellowship.
- ✓ The enemy of God beguiles the unwary by getting mankind to look backwards instead of forwards.
- ✓ God speaks in a still small voice best heard in the quiet solitude of suffering and world's rejection.
- ✓ God is displeased with those that know but do not and less with those who know not and so do not.
- ✓ God's temple is not of bricks and mortars but the heart chosen to be his point of contact on earth.
- ✓ The prism of the old ways distorts the light of God but the lens of the new framed in Christ focuses it.
- ✓ The life circumstances and experiences of every son of God will mirror the profile of Christ.
- ✓ Every attack of the enemy that the believer withstands leads closer to the heart of God.
- ✓ The cross that the faithful endure in compassion with Christ is the bridge into the eternal realm.
- ✓ The sons may suffer in the world but God's doting love proves more than enough to heal their pain.

The surreptitious wields an evil streak

With undercurrents to tow man down

In emotions ever as fickle as the wind

To flood the mind with passing fancies

Chapter 17

LOVE THAT ASKS FOR LITTLE

Grace is borne of goodness sake from love that asks for nothing in return and may be likened to the lifeblood that sustains the body of Christ. On the other hand, mercy is provision availed to the body of Christ by a 'Grand' entity outside of the fellowship but connected to it in spirit. Put simply, the body is nourished within by grace but provided from without by mercy. It is within the framework of grace that believers are sustained during spiritual immaturity and that of mercy that they ask to receive in maturity.

Wherever there is lack of grace, the body is devoid of the spirit of new life in Christ. Such a body is spiritually dead but plods along under the weight of the old self through a process of fission or self-cannibalism where the parts of the body devour each other. It is a hotbed of self-defeating activities that ends in spiritual death. It may look like a feast to the blind in spirit but it is really the macabre dance of maggots in a celebration of the dead and dying. By contrast, wherever grace abounds the body is filled with the spirit of new life. It is alive and abounds fully by a process of fusion where parts reach out to each other in cross pollination to create new life. It is a joyful feast not of eating and drinking in the flesh but of thriving in a spirit of goodness. It is indeed a life of milk for therein the new is borne and sustained. It is of honey as well because the parts fuse in love to produce the sweet nectar of new life.

The life that lacks grace makes itself evident in many ways. He that lacks grace has difficulty in giving thanks and showing appreciation. He is always on the defensive and cannot ask for forgiveness easily. He is wise in his own eyes and cannot ask for or welcome good counsel. He is prone to blaming and finding fault with others. He is easily provoked and lacks peace within. He is righteous in his own eyes and given to manipulation so as to win the approval of others. He does his 'good deeds' only when there is an audience to laud him with praise. He may be a professor of faith but he is not a true confessor for he feels exposed in pure light of Truth. He is a purveyor as well as a victim of such lies that masquerade as Truth. Beyond all that, such cannot perceive the 'hidden' things of God for he is a blind man that plods along in a world of darkness.

Wherever the true word of God is faithfully shared is a table of true enlightenment. It is a feeding trough where the sheep of the flock are nourished with the word of life. The word shared and laid out for the flock in Truth is good nourishment for the spirit. He who feeds worthily will be transformed in light of the spirit of the words that he has received in good faith. He that receives in good faith will lay up the words in the treasure chest of his heart. What one eats becomes him or one becomes what he eats. Either way, he will grow in the spirit of God or the spirit of God will grow within him. In the same vein, the follower after Christ will apprehend him or Christ will apprehend the faithful follower in due time. In time there will be no distinction between the two for the seeker will become an organic 'representation' of the spirit of God. He will become an embodiment of the spirit of God to always speak from the abundance of that which is laid up in his heart. In that case, the heart has become a holy place from which Truth is faithfully offered up in loving faith.

Wherever there is Truth, the light of God shines brightly. Being in the light of God brings about an enlightenment that cures spiritual blindness. When spiritual blindness is cured sight returns and one can see which way to go. He who knows which way to go is no longer 'lame' for he can then go freely on his merry way. The power and mystery of Christ is made possible with a healthy dose of grace. He that embraces Truth in love will be duly filled with grace. Where grace abounds is where the Spirit of God abounds also. The faithful that abounds in grace will be shielded from the traps of the prince of darkness. But he that has rejected Truth has not made room in his heart for grace to abound and for the spirit of God to find welcome. He will lack the wherewithal necessary for victorious living and will not be able to escape entrapment by the enemy. Grace is necessary for victorious living in the world and is availed to the seeker through the light of Christ. It is only through Christ that answers can be found to overcome the world and reconnect with the heavenly Father.

He through whom Truth is declared to reveal the hidden has become an exalted spiritual being. In effect, he has become an oracle through whom God speaks to mankind. Every oracle of God has been equipped as a precious vessel dully fitted to serve God and humanity in love. Through this calling on his life, such is given to impact many lives and change surroundings through the light of Christ infused in his words. Oftentimes the burden feels heavy and the work seemingly overwhelming but he that is truly called will always finds strength to carry on. It is in this light that the oracle of God diligently tends the earthly garden that God has appointed for him for therein is his victory ordained. Every such gardener is given to make the world better as he changes the human landscape with his words so that light may spread to help beclouded eyes.

Every true vessel of God is called to model a better way for the people whose eyes tradition has clouded. The way of tradition is surreptitious in that it aims to boast and vaunt self. But the new way of Christ is truthful, does not exalt self and eschews boasting. Only God is honored and exalted in the new way of Christ. Christ takes mankind into a bright future whereas the old way of tradition returns him to a dark past. The old way is emblematic of the serpent which molts and covers itself with new skin yet remains the same within its unchanging ugly heart. It prides itself in material things to spawn a culture of thievery, misappropriation and unaccountability. It is a cesspool where might assumes to be right and the wrong seems so strong. Every vessel that serves God truly hates the way of the world that the faithless love. He hates it when the creature mocks his Creator with his hypocritical and pretentious ways. He hates it for he knows that it breaks God's heart as he sees his beautiful creation earth marred with such ugliness and disregard for justice.

The true vessel of God does not hate the people but the way of spiritual ugliness that they have chosen. He that serves God truly loves the people so much that he is willing to lay down his life to journey to the distant and foreign land of Truth. The essence of that foreign land is the good and perfect that brings fulfillment. Every true vessel is a custodian of divine gifts who returns to share in love with those hearts willing to receive. It is by the true vessels that misguided hearts in the darkest of places get a chance to partake in or at least have a taste of the glorious availed in divine light.

Such is glory that is not boastful but dignified in hushed

splendor. It is the glory of the flower in spring blossom. It is the glory of the bird that sings because it is free to live and love. It is the glory of the eagle that soars in its audacious hope to touch the sky. It is the glory of the morning dew that covers all things with the wet kisses of life. It is the glory that mortal man once knew but lost in a faraway place called Eden.

God affords his true vessels such glory and protects them through their earthly journey. Every such vessel is a lover of Truth and an emissary of light who is willing to suffer in love to serve God's purposes. As such, his handwork will shine with distinction for God uses every vessel to accomplish the works of glory. The heavenly Father who created all has anointed such vessels among all peoples.

Within each race, color, tribe and tongue is a true vessel so chosen and christened in divine light for the people. There is always one christened in true light that is woven from the fiber of the people's lowly Nazareth. It is so because God has made provision so that every man can have a chance to meet or have knowledge of the true. Sadly, most men will meet them but never come to know such chosen vessels for who they are. It is not on account of oversight by Heaven. It is on account of spiritual blindness that bedevils mankind borne out of not seeking after God sincerely and not fully embracing the light of Christ.

Oftentimes the chosen vessel of light may not be openly acknowledged for who he is and may not be fully aware of the transformation that he has brought about among the people. For that reason, he may think that he has failed in his mission of bringing true light to rid the darkness within the hearts of the people. However, some do come to know without a doubt that a man for all ages has been woven from the cloth of their lowly Nazareth. They will know that a noble spirit has been wrought from where nothing good was expected to come. Every such vessel is used to show the true way so that those that sincerely seek can find it but the journey is always long and wearying.

The honey is not tasted before or during the battle but after victory has been secured. And so, the testimony of every chosen vessel will be enduring for his way will come to be desired and sought after by the people long after his work is done on earth. Each chosen vessel has embarked on the long great journey to divine glory where Truth nourishes the soul and sustains the spirit. Such are travelers among an innumerable company of the exalted in spirit that encourage, whisper comfort to soothe troubled souls, and sound the necessary alarm in love.

God uses every chosen vessel to start a new branch in the family tree of the everlasting. He is chosen to raise a tribe of the God fearing and peace loving. Each vessel must not underestimate what God has purposed for his life. Many will follow in his trail to do mighty works in the name of Christ. Every one chosen in this light is given to rear up spiritual children who will stand on his shoulder to do great things. They will carry his mantle to be enabled to see in purer light and be uplifted to greater heights.

The mantle of Christ is a precious gift bestowed by the heavenly Father on every chosen vessel. The mantle focuses the light of the flame and protects the flame of love from being blown out by evil winds of the times. The mantle diffuses the light of the flame so that it can be easy on the eye of the seeker. The mantle enhances the clarity of light yet shields the eye from smoke. The mantle makes possible the transportation of the flame to where it can be of the most benefit. The mantle is divinely woven with threads of grace and covered with the pigment of mercy so that the light of Christ can be well-received. The mantle is what defines every true light for what it is and to crown it for what it serves. The mantle is that which cloaks the enlightened spirit in eternal glory. But the mantle of Christ has to be kept clean and cared for in good faith by faithful obedience to Truth and in patient love.

- ✓ Grace is borne of goodness sake from love that asks for little as the essence of Christ.
- ✓ The man devoid of grace lacks the spirit of life but the faithful abound in it to thrive in goodness.
- ✓ The life that lacks grace is manipulative, self-righteous and always on the defensive.
- ✓ The believer that embraces and lives in accordance with Truth will be filled with essence of the Divine.
- ✓ The believer cured of spiritual blindness will escape entrapment to perceive the wiles of the enemy.
- ✓ The faithful through whom God speaks is a vessel prepared to serve humanity in faithful love.
- ✓ God chooses some so that those in the darkest of places can come to know the glorious and free.
- ✓ There are sons of light for every community but many never know them due to spiritual blindness.
- ✓ The testimony of the emissary of light endures to be sought after long after his earthly work is done.
- ✓ The divine mantle is a precious gift bestowed on the chosen to protect the flame of love within him.

Man that seeks after intimacy with the Divine

Must forget the injustice and hurts of the past

There must be no bitterness found in his heart

As it beclouds the mind to douse love's flame

Chapter 18

ENTRUSTED WITH THE KEY

The season of harvest has ripened for the vessels that live to serve and please God. It is the season of fulfillment for the faithful whose handiworks are well received above. Such obedient vessels that yield to walk in the way that the spirit of God leads now move from victory to victory for the day has dawned when there is great power availed to them to do mighty works. The day has dawned when one man can chase a thousand and when that which takes a thousand days to do can be done in one day. Those for whom this day has dawned do not trust man's judgment but depend on God for guidance, power and strength.

The spirit of God is readily present and his power amply available in this new day for every vessel that is pure of heart. Only those hearts purified in light through Christ who have forgiven past injustices done to them are worthy of use in this new day. Such will get to write a new script in life. The faithful seeker meets up with Christ in the future and not in the past. For that reason, every believer must forget the injustice that has been done to him. There must be no bitterness found in him for such beclouds the heart to dampen the flame of love therein. He must let go of the past for he seeks after a new life in a new place. He must leave vengeance and judgment to the God of justice whose timing is always perfect. The tribulations of the past serve to prepare and strengthen faith in God through Christ. The faithful seeker must keep his eye on the prize ahead for he that returns to the places of the past can neither meet up nor keep up with Christ. He that has met up with Christ gets to stand under the mercy of God. For that reason, he must remain in the instant for he has become a son of 'today' who must be ready at all times to answer God's call to service. All great things appointed to be accomplished through Christ take place in the future and not in the past which holds no stake under mercy.

Indeed, it should be noted by every seeker that Providence lies ahead for those that seek in Truth after Christ. Divine gifts can only be realized through Christ when mankind opens his heart fully to Truth. However it takes the spirit of God to induce mankind to open his heart to heed. He that yields to the impulse of the spirit in such moments will hear some hidden but convincing truth that God has set aside for him to receive. Such are words communicated in truth and love through the speaker but directed to pierce through the guard walls of the listener's heart to reach his spiritual core. There are made known so that the listener will have little doubt that God is trying to reach him. All who are entrusted with such hidden knowledge are shooters of golden arrows which never miss their mark.

The hidden truths are words of knowledge and insight needed to address every situation encountered in life so that the best outcome can result. Such are words used to turn lemons into lemonade or better yet water into wine. He that is able to receive such knowledge has received the means to overcome and be victorious in life. He will have the words to reach men's hearts and pierce even the hardened ones. In effect, he can break the stony heart with his words to plant the seed of Christ therein in good faith with love. It takes such to induce the man with the hardened exterior to yield and allow the good within to show forth. He that can be used in this way is one divinely equipped to uplift those flattened by life's troubles and help reshape them into vessels worthy of use by God.

The faithful that is privy to hidden truths is given to do the marvelous in the sight of men to the praise and glory of God. Such is a custodian of the key words that unlock life's knots. He is given to live the life of the mysteries in the way of Christ for he has been purified in the dew of Truth and covered with the mist of life. Divine wisdom will crown his life with eternity marked as his final destination. Such is one who takes little for himself for he knows that he is passing through to a better place and so has no need for much on earth. It helps to think of him as a ghost that passes through the night time of the earthly experience who leaves a trail of enlightenment that changes the landscape for better in his wake wherever he has been.

To whom much is given is one from whom much is expected and to whom much is committed from him much is required. He that receives the heavenly gifts must do so with thanksgiving to God who gives good gifts in mercy. Such must never neglect to share or remain humble for he is only a vessel used to render reasonable service to the Creator and creation. Without the humility engendered through thanksgiving, mankind is prone to become vain and consequently unfulfilled within. The faithful cannot afford not to be humble for it is a divine disposition. Humility is the precursor as well as an invitation to goodness and mercy. The word 'please' is crucial for keeping the fountain of grace open. Lack of appreciation or not showing thankfulness shuts off the fountain. The word 'please' maintains the right hand in good use and keeps it from withering. The word 'please' makes the possession of the good and perfect gifts to be expedient for such are received with the right hand of gratitude.

The gifts received from the heavenly Father must not be abused but used for good service. He that does so will receive even more but he that does not will be denied. 'Please' is a word revered by the honorable but it is a strange notion for the violator in spirit that desires to take by force. The good gifts are given freely by the Father but such are not free. The honorable knows that he has life and due knowledge because God allows it. He knows that he has possessions because God makes ample provision for him. He is content in such knowledge and therefore boasts not in self accomplishments but in Christ.

He that is privy to the hidden truths is given to plow with the full yoke of the oxen of Israel with thanksgiving to God always. He is given to walk in the fullness of the riches of God through Christ. He will be like one that carries the mantle to set ablaze the flame of Christ. He will be the spiritual son in whom the Father is perfected. The full blessing of Israel will rest upon him so that he will have power both with God and with men. The spirit of God will be readily present and divine power mightily available through him. The invisible hand of God will always guide him to perceive opportunities where other men see none. He will receive favors where others are denied and have access to the third that only the sons can have. The curse of the serpent will be lifted from wherever he treads and in whatever he touches for he has been sanctified in Truth.

He that has set his hands to plow in the kingdom of God must not look back. The spirit and power of God have an exceptional utility quotient that serves humanity in countless ways through all areas of life. Divine power has the limitless potential to make, break or change things for better in the life of the believer. God is not to be resisted but yielded to. His power cannot be conjured up but tarried for. He chooses the vessel that he deems to be worthy of use. He chooses the faithful that will not hinder but allow his purposes to be accomplished on earth. Divine power is given to overcome myriad obstacles but partial to the humble, meek and truthful.

He whom the spirit of God deems worthy to be used in this light is of immense service to Heaven and earth. But he must always seek to please God and not men. He must tarry for the spirit of God to prompt him to perform his reasonable service as one who dwells in the congregation of the just. The latter is for the pure of heart and therein divine illumination orders footsteps. There is always ample room in the congregation for all who are willing to trust and obey in good faith. There is little worry there but peace within for all who tarry to heed the Master in good faith. Such is a desirable place that only a few find as it is not for those who seek after the praise of men. Those who seek after the praise of men dwell in partial light and shadowy places where the spirit within is often famished.

The divine spirit is the auto pilot who sets the course for those that dwell under the peace and light of Christ. The course must never be changed by the faithful for it has been set on a pre-determined course. He that follows the pre-set course will come into the knowledge of all things for he walks on the golden trail where mankind is given to search out the hidden truths. Every believer is judged by what he knows and lives by. It is a sin to have knowledge of Truth and not obey same. Many have no knowledge of Truth and therefore know not what to obey. Indeed there will be many stripes for those who know and obey not but little for those who know not what they do. Divine wisdom and knowledge are availed freely but such come with responsibility as well as accountability.

There is always a surreptitious spirit sent by the prince of the darkness of this world to tempt the pure of heart that dwell in the light of Christ. The enemy knows that the pure of heart have loving and giving hearts with no guile to be found therein. And so, the prince of darkness comes to entrap the faithful with feigned love embodied in the seductive spirit. But it is the kind that poisons the water. It looks lovely on the outside but it is ugly within. It is darkness that masquerades as light to becloud the mind and corrupt the seed of the great things that God has in plan for the faithful. The latter must remain separated from that which defiles the vessel for there must be no unequal yoking in Christ as it hinders the work of light.

Only the few who partake worthily of grace are nourished and sustained in spirit to meet up with Christ. Only those that have met up with Christ receive the key of knowledge to be able to search out the hidden truths and mysteries of the kingdom. He that has the key will be tuned to hear and understand with clarity. He will see and perceive the true nature of all things. The words of scripture will be framed into pictures wherein he will find himself because he has been adopted into the family of God. Scripture is really about good news and hope of the everlasting for mankind through Christ. He that has met up with Christ has become a son as well as one who will see self and life reflected throughout the scriptures. The things concerning Christ will fit the profile of his life for the sons share a common template that remains unchanging through time.

The key of knowledge and true understanding is never given to the profane for such will abuse it. It is for the righteous before God who live not for self but in love for all. The key of knowledge unlocks the secrets of the kingdom and creation itself. It unlocks the secret of the plain and unassuming manna that sustains the weary traveler through adversity. It unlocks the secret of Aaron's rod that has an everlasting covenant with life. It affords the key to the possessor to untie many of life's problems that bedevil humanity. However he that is entrusted with the key must think kingly thoughts and take princely steps in his earthly journey for he is judged by a higher standard.

- ✓ He that serves God faithfully is always victorious in life for the Spirit of God accompanies him.
- ✓ Hidden truths are 'whispered' into faithful hearts and are used to bring about needed changes.
- ✓ Divine wisdom affords knowledge to break the hardened heart and mold such into a vessel of God.
- ✓ The faithful always leaves a trail of enlightenment that changes the human landscape for better.
- ✓ The faithful receive heavenly gifts under mercy with due acknowledgements to God always.
- ✓ Grace is revered by the honorable but a strange notion for violators that desire to take by force.
- ✓ The blessed see opportunities where others see none and receive favors where others are denied.
- ✓ The potential of the power of God to make, break or change things for better has no limits.
- ✓ The Spirit of God sets the course and guides the steps of those that walk in the peace of Christ.
- ✓ Feigned love is used by the enemy to becloud the mind and forestall God's good plans for mankind.
- ✓ The seeker that has met up with Christ will see his life reflected through the words of scripture.
- ✓ The righteous before God live not for self but in love for humanity and goodness.

Humility is well-acquainted with the Divine

For it is the essence of life and the enduring

The humble will always be worthy of honor

For Heaven embraces and never resists such

Chapter 19

NEW GIFTS AND SKILLS

For all intents and purposes, the very young in faith may be likened to fish that have just been pulled out of the darkened sea of worldliness. If such remain obedient in Christ, they will go on to become like fish broiled in the fire of Truth. The broiled fish is the faithful believer who has been baptized in the fire of the spirit of Christ. He is one who has willingly offered up self as a living sacrifice in the way so as to come into communion with the Divine. He is the diligent seeker given to meet up with Christ and duly join the congregation of the sons of God. He will become a congregant of the living church of Christ with a passport into the kingdom of God. All who have this passport of life can fish other men out of the sea of the world on to the path of redemption in accordance with divine will.

He that has met up with Christ will come into profound knowledge of the ways of God and be enabled thereby to experience the Divine in remarkable ways. He will become privy to sacred knowledge revealed only in true light to those pure of heart. The sacred pertains to the mysteries by which the sons of God battle victoriously against spiritual wickedness and darkness in the world. The young believer that has been set on the path of redemption must continue thereon with due diligence. He must remain obedient to Truth so that he can grow into certainty of faith in due time to come into knowledge of the mysteries and power of God through Christ.

The early years of faith are the most perilous for the slopes up God's mountain are very slippery. It is highly necessary in that season to live true to the sincere milk of the word so that the young roots of faith can remain nourished. When the roots of faith are nourished and established, the faithful believer will grow from milk to be able to eat the meat of the word as well as experience rebirth in Christ. However there are myriad temptations and great trials to overcome before this can come about. Rebirth in Christ is availed through grace and fully realized as the seeker matures spiritually to stand before God under mercy.

Redemption of soul and salvation in eternity with God do not come by mankind's efforts but as a divine gift received freely through grace. The young believer must persevere through the difficult circumstances and trials of the early years so that he can meet up with Christ to realize redemption and salvation. He must forego much in the way as necessary so that in time he may become a son that stands before God under mercy. All knowledge obtained in seeking after Christ remains invaluable and true for all times. Nothing is wasted in seeking after Christ for what precedes serves as the basis from which the new emerges. The more the believer learns and keeps of Christ is the more that he is transformed into divine likeness. At full transformation, he will become one with Christ as a son well prepared to serve God in true light for all ages.

He that strives to be faithful in his spiritual walk must be willing to lay down his life for others as called for it is what frames Christ. He must be willing to accept all who come to him in search of Truth. He must be willing to accept all such as his spiritual charge. It must be that way if he desires to be fully baptized in the fire of the spirit of God. The spirit of God will never depart from him that has been baptized in Truth. The latter cannot be reversed and the gifts associated with cannot be revoked. God will not repent or change his mind about the gifts that come with baptism in the fire of Truth. It may be withheld for a season such as dams and locks control the flow of a river. However it is eventually released to serve its purpose in accordance with God's purposes. He that has been baptized in the fire of Truth will duly pick up his life again in full flourish to be divinely led into the newer and better.

The believer that has been baptized in the fire of the spirit will awaken to a new reality in Christ. He will find that he has become a different creature from what he used to be. He must therefore resist the tendency to return to where and what he has left behind. He will be disappointed if he attempts to do that for he will not find satisfaction in it. But in time he will come to find that the glory of the new that is now available to him through God is far greater than that of the old which must be left behind. He must reach out and embrace his new life in Christ fully. He that has been transformed in this light needs time to understand his new reality. It takes time to understand the scope and full nature of rebirth in divine likeness. The scope of services available to the reborn is a lifelong odyssey of discovery for such will no longer do things by his might or power but in the spirit of God. His requests will become readily granted in mercy and his conversations will cease to be of the lowly and worldly but of the purer and heavenly.

He that has been baptized in the fire of the spirit is bestowed with clarity of mind that enables him to be in tune with creation. He will gain a sense of orderliness that will dictate to him where things around him should be and what purpose they should serve. It is this sense of the nature of things that leads the faithful to get rid of the cumbersome in life. He that has clarity of mind can search out the important that matters in his life and environment.

Such is the nature of the new awakening in Christ for it

brings better understanding in purer light and hope that makes much possible for the believer. He that has been awakened fully in this light will come to discover that he is able to do certain things exceedingly well. Such is the ability of divine power to induce special gifts that had not been demonstrated before to surface from within everyone that is reborn in divine light.

It takes some time for the reborn in light to realize and fully understand that divine power availed through Christ makes the ability to do many things possible. Such must take time to take stock of all the gifts and skills that the spirit of God has induced to surface through him. The gifts usually add up to point in a clear and definite direction for his life. All the gifts are components that assemble into a divinely appointed vehicle that will carry him through the rest of his life as he serves God and goodness. The time invested by the believer to pray and take stock of his life in this wise will be highly rewarding. It will allow him to be able to recognize the new direction in which God is leading him for he has embarked on the sweet ride to glory.

He that has been baptized in the fire of the spirit will find out that everything left in his life has a destined purpose. He will find that all that he needs in his new life has been provided for. It will amaze him to find that everything now works out for good for him. He must therefore strive for perfection in all that he does as life has become about the spirit of God doing the marvelous to behold through him. He must leave no room in his life for the un-needed and un-necessary but make more room in his heart for the lovely that is of a good report so that the spirit reborn within him can flourish in glorious service.

With the awakening of new life in the faithful, he will come to better know the roles destined for all that 'flock' to his side. He will come to know what divinely ordained part each has to play within the fellowship of Christ. All who embrace their roles will flourish but those who reject same will be left out of the divine design. There should be no attempt to mix the old with new life in Christ. The faithful should not attempt to resurrect his old life. He should nail the door of his old life shut and stride boldly into the open door of his new life in Christ. He must resist the urge to patch his old life on to the new. The old and new lives are different entities that do not mix well and do not match. There are to be kept apart for God's blessing is never realized in discord or confusion. The divine blessings abound fully when all parts are in harmony. The wine of the new life in Christ takes some time for the taste to be acquired but it turns out to be gloriously sweet in the end. But it is sweetness and blessing only realized by those willing to go where God sends and to do as he commands.

True enlightenment comes about by faithfully feeding and living in accordance with God's word of Truth. The feeding should not only take place during the times of prayer and study. Every moment in life is an occasion to learn about God if the believer is tuned in spirit to hear. God uses everything and every moment to teach the faithful about his way. All who reach out for the word of Truth must feed worthily for it is offered in love. It is bread of life that duly turns into the meat of the spirit. It is the meat of the spirit that makes for strong faith and affords the key of knowledge. Where the true bread of the word is faithfully broken and shared, certain truths that had hitherto been hidden thereabouts will be revealed. Such knowledge is duly revealed from a spiritual realm beyond mankind's flesh in moments of divine inspiration to bring the faithful into a greater light of understanding.

Greater understanding lifts up mankind's spirit higher to a place closer to the heart of God. He that is lifted up there can see as well as know better in purer light. The uplifted in spirit will acquire a heavenly perspective and be able to hear the still small of the Holy Ghost that affords the faithful comfort. The Holy Ghost whispers from heavenly places into the heart of the faithful to affirm the spiritual connection between God and man. 'He' is given to bring due knowledge so that the faithful can be prepared as necessary to deal with every situation and circumstance that he encounters in life. It takes such knowledge to help make the hills low, fill up the valleys and straighten the crooked for the faithful. The words of the Holy Ghost issue forth from the throne of the heavenly Father and have great capacity to change things for better as there are given to ameliorate life's circumstances. The words must be heeded once received as circumstances are changed for good when such are taken to heart and acted upon.

The Holy Ghost can only be received by the pure of heart for 'he' brings knowledge that is not to be profaned or used for selfish gain. The words of the Holy Ghost will not accomplish anything unless it is acted upon. The Holy Spirit is the medium which enables action in the faithful believer. It takes the Holy Ghost in conjunction with the Holy Spirit for the believer to accomplish the works of glory. The lust for material things is a dense fog that beclouds the mind to tune out reception of the Holy Ghost while the lust of the flesh is a choke that hinders the flow of the Holy Spirit. In effect, hunger after materials and the lust of the flesh limits the effectiveness of the Holy Ghost as well as that of the Holy Spirit. He that is to be fruitful in the kingdom way must curb his appetite for both the flesh and earthly materials. Moderation in all things makes the spirit to abound and keeps God near but the lust after the worldly keeps all things divine out of hand.

- ✓ The broiled fish is emblematic of the believer who has been washed and purified in the fire of Truth.
- ✓ Those that are obedient to Truth are given to experience divine power in profound ways.
- ✓ True knowledge remains invaluable and enduring as the preceding serves as the basis for the new.
- ✓ He that desires fellowship with the Divine has to lay down his life as called in service of humanity.
- ✓ It is a lifelong odyssey of discovery as the faithful find out the scope of services availed by the Divine.
- ✓ Baptism in fire of the spirit bestows clarity of mind that enables believers to be tuned to creation.
- ✓ The faithful that is baptized in the fire of the spirit will find everything in his life to have a purpose.
- ✓ The baptized in Spirit must strive for the perfect for God will use him to do things amazing to behold.
- ✓ The transformed in spirit must nail the door of his old life shut and stride boldly into the new.
- ✓ Enlightenment comes in flashes of inspiration to bring mankind into greater light of understanding.
- ✓ Greater understanding lifts up the spirit to afford mankind a heavenly perspective about all matters.
- ✓ Lust of the flesh is a dense fog that beclouds the mind to tune out reception of the Holy Ghost.

The new man reborn in greater love

Gets to live in immunity of godliness

For the past has been made impotent

And powerless to harm his golden soul

Chapter 20

IN THE FOOTSTEPS AND HEARTBEAT

The more the believer lives in accordance to Truth is the more that he gets filled with the knowledge and wisdom of God. It is by being faithful and obedient to Truth that mankind can start on the path of spiritual ascension. Spiritual ascension is the figurative mounting up with the wings of the eagle to the exalted realm where the saintly commune with the Divine. The latter is the place where the earthly can rise to meet the heavenly in an embrace of love and comfort. The faithful whose spirit within is able to ascend to that exalted meeting point becomes one who is forever changed. His perspective of the world will never be the same for he will begin to see the total picture and no longer in part as most people do. The total picture comprises both the earthly and the heavenly component of life. He that can see the full picture becomes both circumspective and insightful in all his dealings with his fellow man. He has been given to take the high road for he becomes aware of mankind's shortsightedness and the spiritual blindness of many. Such has become a traveler on the road less travelled that many seek but only a few find. The road less-travelled in this light is the path appointed for the righteous before God where the divine hand is ever near to guide mankind's footsteps.

He that has mounted up with the wings of the eagle will be bestowed with divine wisdom. He that has the vision of the eagle is able to eat the meat of Truth and given to see the picture concealed within things. He can sort out that which matters in life and know to leave the unimportant alone. The lofty spiritual heights to which he soars is the domain of the life bearing rain clouds. Most men, including many who profess to follow after Christ Jesus, trudge along close to the valley spiritually. They traverse the well beaten and familiar tracks. They are not able to mount up to the rain bearing clouds. They intersperse themselves among the low cloud vapors which bear no rain. The low clouds are quickly dispersed hither and thither by the prevailing winds of the times. The low cloud is the milk of the word that is subject to myriad interpretations and by which many seekers of Christ are misled. This area is where many 'churches and denominations' of the world gouge on the spiritually ignorant. All who dwell in the valley will not grow to mature spiritually but will be spiritual dwarfs unable to enter into the kingdom of God.

The life bearing clouds are found high up in the mountains. There are densely pervaded in purity with the dew of life and mists of wisdom. It is a holy place that only the exalted in spirit are allowed into. The mountain is the holy mount of God where only the pure in heart can ascend. He that is able to mount up there is baptized and soaked in the dew of life. The spirit of life will pervade all his being and never leave him. He will become the immortal in spirit who the dew of life follows from the mountain down to the valley as called to do God's work. He can soar up interminably between the mount to soak up the dew and come down again to the valley to bring new life to the parched and thirsty willing to receive. Such has become a rain-man engaged in the eternal dance of the cycle of life performed in sync with the divine heartbeat.

God is always doing a new thing in his never ending process of perfecting man. It is like purifying gold. An assay of one hundred percent purity is hoped for but unattainable because the flesh precludes that. A threshold of ninety percent is acceptable for God's divine purposes. The teaching and words of the Christ Jesus purifies and brings man to the threshold of ninety percent. Beyond that threshold is the new place where the Heavenly Father communes with his sons. It is in the region between ninety and hundred percent that God the Father intermeddles with mankind. It is the place where God seeks out man's company in the cool of the day. The cool of the day is when the sun cannot smite God's chosen ones. It is when the faithful become justified before God and are imputed with Divine righteousness. It is the time appointed for the exalted in spirit to do the glorious on earth as ordained in Heaven. It is in the place of communion between God and the sons that Eden can be found and farmed. It is in the garden where the patriarch and his sons commune that Divine power is showcased. It is the place of the fruitful, fulfilling and enduring fruits where nothing can hide for all things glow in lovely purity.

He that seeks ascension to the exalted heights desires a place on Heaven's tableland and so must be willing to sacrifice everything for love of God. Much like Aaron he must desire to be on God's side always so that his beard and loins will remain covered with the white dew of the divine anointing. He must be willing to make a total commitment to serve with his life and become fitted to offer up sacrifices as well as receive gifts from God on behalf of humanity. He is called to be an elect one that God listens to. He has no past life for his yesterdays are no more. He has become a new man in God by light of Truth imparted through Christ who now has an endless future.

The future beckons the reborn in light through Christ with much hope and promise. He must leave the corruptible and worldly for such are leashes that keep earthbound. To remain free to soar in spirit, mankind must forget the things of the past for there are dead weights that encumber the soul and drag many down. To look back to the mistake-filled past keeps man a victim. But to look to the future makes him to be victorious in life. To be free to soar to the heavenly heights is God's gift to the faithful for therein is ordained the conversation that uplifts humanity. Up there is where mankind becomes privy to the veiled and sacred truths which he must use for the works of divine glory as well as help guide others on to the heavenly path.

He that commits his life to serve God and goodness enters into a covenant with the Heavenly Father. This is the covenant of the son who has left his own worldly pursuits to come home and run the Father's business. This is the covenant of Christ. The Father's business is to show the children of the valley who dwell in the shadows how to soar in spirit to the summit through faith in Christ. The faithful son of covenant is chosen to be the elect through whom the grace of God will flow to those who seek after righteousness. He is the elect of God who has laid down his life to bear the people's infirmities and to carry the scourge of their sins on account of love as well as life. The son of covenant can enter into the veiled place through grace and obtain from God in mercy to share with the needy. He may well be received with doubt, derision and despised by many but time inevitably vindicates him.

The trash of humiliation and rejection piled upon the elect ones affords divine protection. The Father uses the base and despised things of the world to confound those who are wise in their own eyes. The trash of rejection piled on every elect one protects him just as Egypt protected the innocent child of glory from the fury of Herod. The obsolete misguided past remains impotent to harm God's elect ones for they are immunized in godliness and bestowed with goodness as sustenance for the future.

The faithful that is able to ascend from the valley to the summit of God's mountain has joined the divine family. He has embarked on the journey of the deified in spirit who walks among men but dwells in spirit with the Heavenly Father. Though his spirit soars to the great heights yet he performs his worthy service on earth so that the thirsty garden of humanity's soul may be refreshed in new life. It is a two-step dance. First he offers up sacrifices well-received above through selfless acts on behalf of humanity. Such are the sacrifices well received above for there are not performed for the praise of men but out of a pure heart on account love for God and goodness.

Next the Heavenly Father grants his petitions for he prays in faithfulness with due thanksgiving for what is best and needed for the day. This is the rain dance of life by which the good and perfect gifts are received. The faithful who lives to serve God and humanity in this wise is the true custodian who is diligently rehabilitating Eden from humanity's sunset to its new sunrise. He is one given to reverse the curse of man's yesterdays and replace it with the hopeful promise of tomorrow. He is one who the hand of wisdom guides to erase the mistake of Adam and to replace it with the 'retake' of Christ.

All who can ascend up the mountain of faith live on earth as men but dwell above in spirit within the congregation of the justified before God through Christ. By them and in them, Christ is very well alive and carrying on the Heavenly Father's work on earth. By them the walls of darkness are being torn down so that divine light can shine into men's hearts all over the world. Only such can declare boldly that Christ has come alive for they know that he has come to full life within them.

When Christ has come to full maturity within the devoted believer, he emerges from within when the occasion arises to lead him forward in his earthly walk. He emerges so that the misguided past of the yesterdays can be severed and the full promise of tomorrow can be realized. The yesterdays of life attempt to hold back from the promise of the future. The yesterdays of life are the hurts and wounds of broken promises. There are the disappointments of unfulfilled dreams. The wounds of yesterday though buried deep within can be soothed and healed by the balm of the divine anointing through Christ. Only Christ can soothe the wounds of life so that they no longer define the faithful believer. Christ emerges from within to urge the faithful to fear not but come along to rendezvous with the Divine and destiny's fulfillment. Christ emerges to lead into Providence where man's true destiny is manifested and realized. Christ within emerges to lead so that the faithful can finally stand firm to be counted among the righteous.

It is by faithfulness that the believer learns to banish his fears. He in whom Christ has come to full life no longer has anything to fear but must set his mind on the things above. There is no fear up above where the spirit is free to excel. Where there is no fear, love is perfected and abounds. It is only in the exalted heights as man becomes truly focused on the Heavenly that he can realize the perfection of godliness ordained for him. There are no yesterdays to be found in the starry heights but the limitless expanse of tomorrow. The clusters of grace are found on the lower branches of the tree of life but the choice grapes of mercy are obtained on the uppermost boughs. The faithful believer is nourished through the fears of his infant days with the cluster of grace in the lower branches. But when Christ comes to full maturity, he can reach up to the uppermost boughs to find the choice and tender grapes of mercy that abound there.

- ✓ The believer that lives in faithfulness to Truth will be duly filled with knowledge and divine wisdom.
- ✓ The lofty realm to which the faithful soar in spirit is the domain of new life.
- ✓ The believer able to ascend up the Holy mount of God will be baptized and soaked in the dew of life.
- ✓ God is long suffering and does new things for the perfection of the faithful in an unending process.
- ✓ The faithful reborn in full light has no past for his yesterdays are no more but his future is endless.
- ✓ The past things are dead weights that drag down the spirit and preclude the promises of the future.
- ✓ The scorn, humiliation and rejection of the faithful afford divine immunity in the long-term.
- ✓ The faithful that serves humanity in the light of true love is a kindler of the embers of Hope.
- ✓ God uses the elect to tear down walls of darkness so that divine light can shine through for all.

Songs that swell in thankful hearts

In voices tuned to praise in grace

Lift mankind on the wings of joy

Into a realm of sunshine and love

Chapter 21

UNDER SUNSHINE OF LOVE

❦

The believer does not begin his walk with God full of faith. It takes some time to learn to fly on the wings of faith. It takes some time to realize the fullness of riches that faith in God avails through Christ. It takes some time to un-wrap the burial bandages of Lazarus and step out as the fully matured in spirit reborn into full light. He that is fully matured in Christ has become a son of God in heavenly light and will remain so for all ages. Nothing in Heaven above or earth below can separate such from the love of God for he has obtained an irreversible gift. The Heavenly Father will make a cleft so that he can be grafted to the Divine and be able to possess all that his heart desires.

For the faithful believer to be engrafted to the Divine he has to undergo a process of sorting out his life so as to weed out the un-necessary and make room for only the necessary. The pruned life has a lot of re-building to do. But things have to be done in a better light so that there is nothing left to clutter or encumber life. When this is done, he will discover with much joy that his petitions and hearts desires will always be met. The faithful whose heart's desires are readily fulfilled has to set his mind to the lofty standards pleasing to God. It has to be that way so that he can become a 'projector' that makes heavenly things to be realized on earth. He must always have a 'to-do' list that is impressed on his heart. The Spirit of God will search out the items on his 'to-do' list and help to make them come about to his delight. He must make sure that the items on his 'to-do' list will be of a good report before Heaven and earth. If that is the case, then he will find that all that he needs to do will always be carried out to completion. Such a faithful one must make sure to carry out only those 'projects' that serve the cause of godliness and goodness well. If he does that faithfully, he will find that things will be less taxing and expediently done. The days of struggles, shortfalls, short changes and disappointments will be gone.

The season and years of tribulation are divinely ordained to serve the goal of engrafting the believer into the divine stream and will cease once that has been accomplished. They can never be regeneration without tribulation. Before regeneration the faithful believer labors with his mind and flesh. But that will never be enough for all his efforts and endeavors will always fall short of bringing the desired results. The vehicle of that earlier life often disappoints and strands on the way. It can never climb to the top of victory hill or drive out of the miry clay of disappointment valley. But then in regeneration, all things become possible and expedient through the power of the spirit of the Almighty.

The faithful that has come into regeneration has entered into faith-rest with the Heavenly Father. He will find that the vehicle of his life has been retooled into an all-weather utility transport fit for every terrain of life. Such is called to use the retooled vehicle to harness the sunshine of Divine love to do amazing things. He must use the power of that divine sunshine for victorious service on earth to benefit all who are willing to embrace Truth in love. He has become a 'bee' prepared for the propagation of new life through Christ and so has a lot of honeycombs to make to feed those who will be drawn to him. He is one appointed to be the diligent gardener given to tend the seedlings planted in his earthly lot by God. He must get to work and carry on with it for his time has become precious.

Divine love and power to make things happen on earth are harnessed through the power of prayer and earnest entreaty. The 'bee' needs the sunshine of the Heavenly Father's love to produce the pleasing and fulfilling potion of honey. The son that asks not receives not but he that asks will receive in fullness of joy. Such that has come under the sunshine of divine love will enter into rest. The latter is appointed for those received into the company of a host of spiritual helpers to no longer labor on their own. He must therefore set his mind on such things that will exalt him before God. He has become a regenerator and re-creator of the new from the old whose wishes are his divine helpers command. He has become one able to make withdrawals from the Heavenly vault to make new things appear on the earthly plane.

The spiritual helpers are there to provide roadside service as well as other needed help so that the faithful that is in faith rest can never be stranded on the way again. The helpers maintain, harvest and pack the fruits of his labor in the twinkling of an eye so to say for time seemingly appears to become compressed for the faithful in faith rest. Time indeed appears to stand still for the man that can do a lot in little time. This is because in regeneration God pre-positions the building blocks needed to build the new life ordained for the believer through spiritual helpers. Such will find the seeds of the things that he needs for his fulfillment available and made affordable to him. He is one that has come to the parkway of life where the way is made expedient for the faithful. It is on this parkway during regeneration, that the hills are made low, the valleys filled and the crooked made straight under the sunshine of divine love.

God knows the earthly state of all who are in faith-rest and wants to show every son that he is much beloved. Therefore the Heavenly Father readily displays his power through them. He wants to show the sons that the world is indeed his creation. He that has come into faith-rest has come into the place of favors and must affirm this truth by modeling his life after Christ. He must speak and live as the son of Heaven that he has become. Every son of Heaven is a copy of Christ Jesus in his inner man. The Christ 'borne' within each son of Heaven is not readily known for many are spiritually blind and dim of soul to perceive. But Truth cannot be buried for he that is alive in every son of Heaven comes to be known in due time. The burial bandages of Lazarus take some time to be un-wrapped. As the bandages are progressively un-wrapped, the fullness of what God has wrought in each son and purposed for him becomes more evident. All who truly seek after Christ will come to know and embrace the sons for they are permeated with the essence of the Divine. All who are not spiritually 'blind' will see that the handiworks of the sons glow with purity and that divine glory shrouds them.

The handiworks of the faithful in faith-rest are like honeycombs that showcase and bring the wisdom of the Divine into display before mankind. All such handiworks are modules which fit together into a grand whole that embodies the sustainable, fulfilling and enduring. The totality of such handiworks paints a glorious picture that unfolds with the passage of time. The honeycomb is the product of cross-pollination and blending of many parts into one pleasant whole. He that can produce the honeycomb will raise many fruitful trees. He will always have the veil of the hidden parted for him. The hidden truths are seminal seeds for the advent age of the new heaven on earth. He that is privy to them has become connected to the Divine mind and chosen to help shape the future of the earth in the similitude of Heaven. He that is so connected lives in God even as the Heavenly Father lives in him to have charity govern all his actions.

Charity is the universal umbrella that covers the faithful believer in faith-rest as he carries out his calling on earth. Charity is a strong advocate for justification before God. It leads mankind to live so that others may come to learn about the divine way. God favors the charitable in spirit and makes necessary pre-arrangements to uphold such in the work ordained ahead for them on earth. He that is in faith-rest never walks in blindness but rather is willing to tarry for Divine guidance in all endeavors. Such never forgets that he no longer labors by his own flesh but in the spirit of the living God. For him patience is not only a virtue but highly necessary. The faithful in faith rest walks under divine sunshine and so must maintain what he has received in truth, humility and thanksgiving to God. He must nurture and use his gifts well for he has been received into the company of exalted souls. He is called to maintain the 'vehicle' that he has received so that it must remain ever ready as needed for he has embarked on a great journey in service of God and humanity.

The vehicle powered by divine sunshine is not limited but universal. It can go any and everywhere as duty calls and love urges. It is the vehicle of the purified soul riding on the Divine Spirit. It can travel to wherever needed in the light of Truth and instant of time. Therefore such must not be concerned with the worldly but with serving the Heavenly Father's will for which he has been prepared. The worldly embody the weighty and encumbering which are dead weights that ground the vehicle and limit its readiness to serve. Grounding the vehicle defeats its universal purpose for then the faithful believer can no longer do all things through Christ as he has been empowered to. In that case, the believer that should have been free to soar freely among the exalted becomes a 'groundhog' trapped in the futile dreariness of an endless loop. Therefore it must be strongly emphasized that the vehicle of 'the purified soul that rides on the divine wind' given to the faithful under divine sunshine must always be maintained for good service by using it wisely and charitably to make humanity better.

The snapshot of the purified soul that rides on the divine wind taken through the lens of the world often shows one who is not easily categorized. He does not belong anywhere completely yet he belongs everywhere in part. The world may see him as incomplete yet he does not lack in any area of life. He is a Samaritan for he is not of one stock but a hybrid of various parts. He is of the circumcision and not of the concision. His circumcision is of the heart and not of the flesh. It is worth pointing out that it is the Samaritan who gets the Truth and ends up on the path of righteousness. It is the Samaritan who will offer up thanks when others will not and who will perceive Christ when many cannot or will not.

He that is seemingly out of place in this world is oftentimes the one whose works are well received by God. Such is like the Samaritan who gets intimated with the wisdom that God is a spirit that must be worshipped in spirit and truth only. Such is like the Samaritan who gets to be intimated with the knowledge that God does not care for ancestry, pedigree or grand cathedrals of worship but seeks after the heart of mankind. Such like the Samaritan will labor in the last days to bring in the last harvests of the souls of men. Such like the Samaritan labors in the spirit of true charity to bind up the wounds of the robbed bypassed by the world. Such like the Samaritan is an outsider in the world but an insider with God given to find life's true treasure by his relationship with the Divine which affords him his heart's desires. Such treasure is the kind that the world cannot take away or thieves steal but availed only when the heart is pure so that mankind can 'see' God.

Only he that is pure of heart can 'see' God. He is not seen in the flesh as men see others. God is everywhere and cannot be localized. Things seen with the eyes of the flesh are localized and therefore limited. God cannot be seen in a location but he can be known. He is known by the spirit and seen through the works of his hand. He is known when he pulses through his chosen ones to inspire feats of creative wonder. He is known when he speaks of things yet to come through the faithful. He is known in the still small voice heard through the ear of the heart in the quiet moments of life. He is known as he hears the cries and responds to the petitions of the faithful. He that can 'see' God is called to lead a kind and peaceable life. He must have compassion for the blindness of those who cannot yet 'see' as he does. He that can 'see' God in wisdom's light is no longer of the kindred of men but of Divinity. He can declare with bold certainty that Jesus Christ is indeed the son of God because he knows it to be true in his heart. He has come to know because he believed, followed and has met up with Christ in the way. The footsteps of Christ have led him to the knowledge of the Father and to share in the gifts reserved for those who live in God even as the Almighty lives in them.

There is always the residue of the flesh that attempts to inhibit the work of the spirit. The spirit is always willing but the flesh is often times weak. It is the heart of man that God seeks after and not his flesh. The heart of the true believer is without guile and purified in Truth. It is duly prepared to be an altar lit with the flame of love. Such is a heart that will always be obedient to the will of God for his desire in life is to please the Heavenly Father. The content of such a heart will be filled with the knowledge and wisdom that lead mankind to realize the fullness of divine riches availed through Christ. The possessor of such a heart is a faithful son whose ways and deeds will remain ever justified before God.

On the contrary, God rejects hearts that are ugly. Spiritual ugliness defines that which appears to be good on the outside but is dark within. The ugly heart engages only in self-serving endeavors orchestrated to earn the accolades and favor of men. The possessors of such are often praised by men who are not able to perceive or know the true contents and intentions of the heart. These hypocrites have perfected the appearance of spirituality and do excel at it. There are purveyors of the leaven of the Pharisees. The ugly heart is devoid of grace and has no share in the commonwealth of Christ. Such is filled with iniquity and wickedness. Iniquity does not use the same standards to make judgments or dispense favors. Iniquity is the inability to see all men as God's creatures for it discriminates and selects. Iniquity spawns the wicked heart which engenders the sacrifice of Truth. The wicked heart disregards conscience to take undue and unfair advantage of others. Both iniquity and wickedness constitute the antithesis of the golden rule which mandates that each man should treat his fellow man as he himself would like to be treated. The ugly heart may fool men for a season but God is never fooled for the handiworks of mankind show up in time to bear witness to the seed within him.

- ✓ The believer does not begin his spiritual journey full of faith and confident in the promises of God.
- ✓ The matured in spirit must set his mind on things above so that he can project the heavenly on earth.
- ✓ Life becomes less taxing and more expedient when earthly projects serve God's purposes.
- ✓ The faithful is like a 'bee' that uses the sunshine of God's love to propagate new life among humanity.
- ✓ The faithful in faith-rest labors not alone for he has been received into a company of spiritual helpers.
- ✓ The faithful that has come to the parkway of life will have healing and restoration effected in his life.
- ✓ The new-man born within the faithful is not readily known in the beginning but shines in due season.
- ✓ The new vehicle given to the faithful is that of his soul riding on wings of the divine Spirit.
- ✓ The sons of God do not belong anywhere completely but belong everywhere in part.
- ✓ God's power works in the sons to inspire feats of creative wonders and evoke sprinkles of wisdom.
- ✓ Spiritual ugliness defines that which appears good on the outside but is evil within.

To hold on to the traditions of the past

When mankind has a foretaste of the new

Precludes him from ascension to the place

Where Heaven has ordered a feast of love

Chapter 22

PERFECTION IN THE SUM

There is a clearly spelt out warning in the Holy Scriptures that implores mankind to be careful not to mock God. Regrettably, this warning which needs to be taken seriously by humanity is mostly treated with disregard by many. Although it has been pointed out countless times that it is not possible to deceive God yet mankind refuses to heed this warning on account of spiritual blindness. Man mocks God in many different ways some obvious and others concealed. The disparaging of scriptures and the blatant disregard for God's commandments is one way. But a more insidious but no less spiteful way is spiritual hypocrisy. Many know and talk about what God requires of mankind but sadly are not able to live as they profess. As a result, religion abounds in many shapes, forms and congregations yet a spiritual famine besets humanity. Evil and wickedness reign in the hearts of many. The young are discouraged by the hypocrisy and injustice of it all. The Heavenly Father who sees and knows all is aware of this travesty of the times. This state of affairs surely breaks his heart without measure and has taken his long suffering patience to the extreme. By mankind's acts of willful disobedience, God's wearied hand of inevitable justice cannot be stayed much longer as mankind has opened the door of doom to his shame and sad regret.

Another subtle but no less harmful way that mankind mocks God is by his persistent and consummate desire to sow in the flesh instead of the spirit. Mankind has become overly enamored with the material. He is not able to understand that man reaps as he sows. Wisdom clearly cautions that he who sows in the flesh reaps corruption but he that sows in the spirit reaps life. The lust for the material leads mankind to cut corners, seek short cuts and compromise Truth. The lust for earthly materials keeps man's soul in bondage and leads him to spiritual death eventually. The soul purified in Truth is lifted up so the spirit can rejoin the source of life from whence it sprang forth. But the soul that is in bondage wallows in the miry clay of the earth and will never rise for lack of life in the spirit. It will remain listless and hunger forever for life but will not find. The Heavenly Father is the source of life. Man's earthly journey becomes meaningless if he is not able to reconcile with the Divine and find everlasting life before his time on earth runs out.

The believer who heeds the teachings of Christ Jesus will grow in knowledge to where his spirit is able to break free of the shackling hold of the earth. His soul will be freed of the bondage of the earth. He will come to reap new life within the divine fold. He will morph into a new creature borne in godliness that lives a spirit led-life more and a flesh driven life less. He will become a spirit-man borne from the old self of his flesh-man. He who continues to sow in the spirit will continue to grow closer to the heart of God. He will gradually be remade in spirit into the full image of his Maker so that it can be said for a fact that he has come home. The reason for the creation of the earth by God is so that it can be used as a nursery for the souls of men. He that is willing to accept 'the garment of the lamb of sacrifice' as his earthly cloak will be gradually remade in the image of the Divine from the base material of his old self. He that has been remade in that image will be able to eat figs from the tree of life and thereby come into knowledge needed for the times.

Man's time on earth should really be about being remade in the spiritual image of the Divine. All the situations and places that the faithful believer goes through in life sum up into the process of remaking him in that light. He that has completed this remaking process will begin to walk on earth under the cloak of Divinity. It is a process of initiation into eternal life and the all-knowing wisdom of God. It is for this reason that Christ Jesus came so that he can model the process for those that believe in him. Anyone that truly follows in the path laid down by Christ Jesus to complete the process will become a 'Christ-Man' who can model the way as well for others who aspire.

During the transformational process a lot of 'pruning' of the worldly takes place in the life of the believer through the unseen hand of God. During those years of spiritual transformation the aspiring believer learns to yield and accept Divine will as the sovereign guide of life. While this takes place, he will be gradually weaned away from the encumbering ways of the world. Those things that are pruned and that he is weaned away from are the unnecessary that inhibit spiritual growth. Those are the weeds which invade the garden of the mind to clutter the soul with wantonness. On the other hand, the seed of life is Truth taught and learned through spiritual experiences in faithfully following after Christ.

Spiritual transformation can be viewed as a distillation process in which the weighty and earthly material sink to the bottom but the light and starry material rise to the top. The weighty material that sinks to the bottom and gets jettisoned is due to the old nature. The light material that rises to the top is borne of the new self through the light of Christ. Only the very important as well as faith in God's goodness are needed for transformation because the path leads upwards where the weighty things impede progress. It is a path of amazement that winds upwards in divinely ordered steps. The believer must trust that God is in control and knows what he is doing. The journey serves to peel away the wrappings of the ego, correct the misguidance of the past and reverse the ravages of time for the faithful. Only the essential core of the spirit remains at the end of spiritual transformation. The core of the spirit is what God is looking for in mankind and that by which he sheds his glory on the faithful. Within that core lies the purified soul of man in which is found the kernel of the Divine. The latter is what God hid in man in the first place and what he comes looking for in the end. It is this kernel which embodies the connection between man the creature and God his Creator.

The more that the believer is purified in spirit is the more that he becomes aware of the reality of God in everything and everywhere. He is in effect getting closer to the source of all knowledge and wisdom in spirit. He is being initiated into a greater understanding where he will begin to understand the universal language of creation. Such a believer will come into a greater and better understanding of what all things in nature are communicating to each other. He is able then to discern all things and nothing of importance can be hidden from him. He is conscious both of the local and the universal issues that pertain to life as one in spiritual communion with the Divine. In effect, he has become a citizen of the universe who lives to serve God more and himself less. He has become a son of Heaven who walks among men under the mantle of divinity. His lot in life then becomes to serve God's will and thereby fulfill his divine purposes on earth.

Those who are reconnected in spirit with the Divine are the proxy through whom God interfaces with humanity.

None others can suffice for this duty except those fully matured in the spirit of Christ. Such hearts are the only ones acceptable to the heavenly Father as points of contact with mankind. These are the true temples of God who as universal spirits look for the things that unite humanity and not such that separate mankind. There is no division and distinction in Christ for his body is a commonwealth of co-sharers. Christ is perfected in the sum of the imperfect parts when and where the veil of darkness has been chased away by the dawn of light. If the different parts are not assembled to fit together, then there is no vehicle to be powered by the Divine. The different parts can never be made to fit perfectly where darkness still exists but only in the pure and true light of God through Christ.

There is but one tradition that all who truly live in Christ observe. The latter are the golden in spirit who come from different backgrounds, cultures and traditions. Such are the faithful ones who have found Christ through living by the golden rule. They seek not after glory for self but after the glory of God through Christ. Such that live by this higher law defy the traditions of men. The traditions of men are borne from that which was fostered at Babel. The traditions of men serve to separate mankind. Traditions are from the past and becloud the eye of the spirit to keep the truth veiled for many. They embody the serpentine that often seduces and beguiles the ignorant into darkness and spiritual demise. He that holds on to the traditions of the past, when he has known the new, will not be able to come up to the feast of love through Christ for he seeks to patch the new on to the old. His spirit will not be fully awakened to be joined to the eternal stream of the Divine.

He that has been bestowed with a universal spirit has left the old ways. Abraham, the father of faith, left the old ways of the old country to begin his journey of faith to a new and far away land. He had not known that land beforehand but the spirit of God led him there regardless. He was not led there in a sprint but in a deliberate and measured way. It had to be that way in order to give him time to break away from the old ways. God takes time to reconfigure the faithful believer in the universal way through patience, obedience and sacrifice. The believer that has the universal spirit is received everywhere. The faithful that has the universal spirit has received the passport that lets him in anywhere. He must watch out for the traps of mankind's traditions and ceremonies. Although these are often times cleverly disguised so as not to appear to be so, there are designed to cater to man's desire to 'make' himself a master and be more than he is. The ways of tradition are designed to make men gloat in their own prowess so others can fawn over them. For man to presume to be a master in the world above others is an ill-conceived and misguided notion. God is the Master of all and those who aspire to be justified before him must live by the heavenly way of the golden rule where all are brethren in the light of Truth and love as God's children.

God is man's Creator and Master. Man has a daunting challenge in attempting to master self by his own devices. It is faith in God that settles the score of life. The man that aspires for mastery in life must rise above the world and go beyond self into the glorious liberty of true light availed through Christ. Only in the reflection of true light can one know true self and thereby come to know his Maker. Once exalted there, he must live to serve God's will and purposes as a co-regent with all the other sons of heaven. It is only through the ladder of faith in God and belief in Christ that the true self can be known to be mastered. He who builds must do so on the sure foundation of Christ. Building on the traditions and ceremonies of man is like building on the quick sands of time as the so-called great civilizations of the past attest. Traditions and ceremonies choose the wisdom of man instead of searching out the true wisdom of God. God's wisdom is ever unfolding, fresh and enduring but man's wisdom becomes stale soon enough. Traditions and ceremonies are devised to praise man the creature instead of God the Creator.

The faithful who can soar to live in glorious liberty is never to be weary in well doing. He must continue in well doing as led in spirit for such works are well received by God and count as treasure stored in the heavenly vaults. Such are works that serve as the seeds of goodness planted for future harvest. The works initiated and enabled by the spirit of God are enduring works that produce good fruits. Such are to be copied and passed on so that the benefits inherent in them can reach all. It makes sense and bodes well for mankind to plant seeds of the Divine with his limited time on earth. The good labor carried out for God and goodness is the only endeavor that will endure in the end when it counts most. On the contrary, the works and labors dictated by the flesh result in dead works. Since dead works are not governed by the spirit but by the flesh, they have no inherent life and so do not endure. Rather such engender envy and contention at the very least. They may look good to the eye in the beginning but fade away sooner or later. They may smell of success for a time but not for long as all things borne of the flesh tend towards decay. At the end, every dead work is just an invitation for maggots to come to feast.

The believer that lives in glorious liberty no longer cares for the works of the flesh. The latter defile and weigh down the soul so that the spirit cannot take flight readily. He that lives in glorious liberty does everything as led in spirit for he has ceased from the works of the flesh. Rather he lives to serve mankind with love and pureness of heart for by such do humanity come to be exalted. He that is led in his endeavors by the Divine is a bearer of precious seeds. He must be firm in spirit so as to remain an acceptable and worthy vessel for use by God. The flesh tends to rear its ugly head occasionally so as to detract the faithful. He that aims to serve God well must let go of many things in order to stay above the world's fray and remain indefatigable in carrying out the work ordained for him. It requires repetitive effort to overcome the pockets of entrenched resistance in the hearts of men. It takes time and diligence to overcome the evil ways of darkness in the world. It is not an easy job with a quick fix but that which must be done with patience, understanding, forgiveness and love.

To convert mankind from the sinful ways of the world is to battle the enemy for the soul of the sinner. It is an exhausting effort that taxes mind, body and spirit. The standard bearer for God must be strong in spirit and fit in body. He must be equipped and geared up for battle at all times. The spread of the kingdom of God happens gradually but steadily. The effective warrior for God must hold his flesh in check in order to be victorious in his battles. He that is called to serve God must live the life of the good shepherd who denies himself so that the beloved flock may abound. He that is a good shepherd often carries deep wounds inflicted by the enemy on account of his faith in God, belief in Christ and love for the flock. But these are only wounds of the flesh for nothing can touch him that has become divine in spirit.

- ✓ Most have an understanding of what God requires of mankind but choose not to live as they know.
- ✓ Mankind's earthly journey becomes meaningless if he is not able to reconcile with God.
- ✓ The faithful that willingly puts on 'the garment of sacrifice' will be duly remade in divine image.
- ✓ Spiritual transformation winds upwards and eschews the material for such drag down.
- ✓ Greater enlightenment affords an understanding of the universal issues pertaining to life.
- ✓ The sons are universal spirits who propagate those things that unite mankind in light and love.
- ✓ The kindness of the golden rule is the one tradition that those who live by divine light observe.
- ✓ The Divine guides the believer in measured steps to afford him time to break away from the old ways.
- ✓ The faithful that seeks to rise into glorious liberty must learn to master the way through Christ.
- ✓ God's standard bearer must be strong in mind, body and spirit so as to be ready for battle always.
- ✓ The good shepherd carries deep wounds as the mark of faithfulness and abiding love.

Love's cord that binds all faithful hearts

Is the concord of praise of joyful tongues

For all in creation that reflect God's glory

Find harmony through acknowledging him

Chapter 23

THE EMBLEM OF HOPE

The believer that diligently feeds on the word of Truth and partakes worthily of grace through Christ will have his old self surely and steadily die. A new man will come alive within him remade in light through redeeming love and divine transformative power. The man of the old nature is earthy and weighty. His destiny is death but the man of the new nature is starry and light. His destiny on the other hand is life in eternity. He that has become transformed in his inner man to become the starry and light has become spiritually buoyant. No longer will he be bound to the earthy for he has overcome the world to find a place among the exalted. Such is one who will prevail over whatever challenges that he encounters in life through faith in God. In effect, the spirit within him has become fitted to pass through anything that stands in his way for he has become a man for all seasons and ages that cares more for the heavenly but less for earthly things.

Man's life on earth can be likened to a ship sailing on the

high seas. There are many who are not able to navigate through the stormy seas of life. Such are like ship-wrecked mariners overcome on life's stormy seas. Their ships are wrecked for lack of proper piloting and a reliable guidance system to warn them of perilous weather ahead. Life is a blind foray into uncharted waters for the ill-informed and oblivious. Such live as fodder for the predatory masterminds of the world who thrive on men's misadventures and misfortunes. Having lived without light for a long time, the spiritually blind do not know better and have become slaves to the prince of this darkness of the world. Most that are spiritually enslaved are creatures of the flesh that love the world too much and have lost their souls therein.

He that loves the ways of the world will hate the ways of God for both are diametrically opposed. The inevitable result of choosing the way of the world is spiritual death that renders mankind's earthly sojourn meaningless in the end. However there are a few able to sail through the world guided by the monitoring system of the divine eye positioned high above. This monitoring and guidance system is the all-seeing and knowing Heavenly Father who dutifully watches over his children on earth. These well-guided ones do not live as most others that are blind do. Rather they take their cue on daily living from the 'eye' above. He that is being guided by the Divine has committed to put his trust in God and serve him. Such a believer no longer labors in his own flesh and for his own gain but is led in spirit to serve God's purpose in all that he does. For such the unseen hand of God will always be near to protect, direct his footsteps and endue him with pertinent knowledge.

He that has the hand of God near to direct his life is distinct in his ways for he has been separated from blind humanity. There is a marked glow that shows from within him for his heart has become an altar lit with the flame of love. This glow is the emblem of hope and comes about as the faithful believer gets closer to the heart of God in spirit. It is the mark of the spirit that has been purified in truth and justified before God. Such a believer has the wellspring of life in him for his mouth will speak forth healing truth abundantly to those willing to embrace. He speaks Truth that is spiritually distinctive from verses of scripture memorized and quoted vainly for self-glory. But the words of Truth that he speaks forth are filled with the essence that breaks stony hearts, encourage faltering steps, feed hungry souls and lift lowly spirits.

Divine wisdom spills forth from him who walks in the light of greater understanding for he has stepped out from the shadowy into full light. Such is one who no longer sees in part but with full clarity and focus. Therefore he will begin to find good and better things with each passing day. There is no end to his amazement for he is given to travel on life's parkway where contentment is found. He will begin to care less for the things of the world as he realizes that his needs are divinely provided for and his wants easily met. Because he finds contentment in that which God provides, he becomes immune to the wear and tear of the world. As a result of that, time appears to slow down for him and age crowns him with graceful wisdom.

The wisdom from above is dispensed on a need to know basis. It is dispensed when the believer has been duly prepared and ready to receive it. Spiritual growth and readiness are realized by diligent study and obedience to the words of Truth. The more that mankind learns about and lives in faithful obedience to the word of Truth, the more the Heavenly Father reveals himself to the seeker. More of the divine nature is revealed when mankind desires and hungers for knowledge on how to come into fellowship with God. Divine wisdom is not dispensed because the believer wants to know but because he needs to know. Each golden nugget of wisdom is given when the due season for that knowledge to be known comes about. Although the Heavenly Father knows all things, he only reveals the needful things to the believer. It is like manna which must be received and eaten fresh each day. God does not haste because he is never late and he does not waste because he always has a good measure of all things. Rather he follows an orderly pattern that is borne of long suffering patience and good hope.

He that has grown to intermeddle with divine wisdom will begin to understand the universal language of all creation.

It is by divine wisdom that the key of understanding to unlock and give insight into all things is received. With such a key the ear of the spirit will begin to hear what everything around is communicating. It is language expressed inaudibly that can be clearly perceived. Although inaudible, it makes mental impressions on the mind when the believer is tuned in spirit to hear it. He that has been bestowed with this key must take the high road in all things in life. The world does not take kindly to such and so he must always seek guidance from above so that he can remain anchored in peace to have his endeavors remain pleasing to God. He must remain focused on the high things that are pleasing to God so that the antenna of the spirit within him can remain in tune with the Divine impulse. On a cautionary note, when the antenna of the spirit wanders and shifts away from the lofty, then the mind inevitably becomes flooded with the distracting stream of the mundane.

He that has received the key of knowledge must guard that which he has received with due care. His lifestyle must change to that of the 'gardener' into whose care are entrusted the precious seeds that are self-contained with the amazing. He must have the patient wisdom to cultivate and bring out the rare things which have been preserved in those seeds by the Divine. He must master the call that makes life to rise up from sleep and the entombed to spring forth in freedom's dance. He is one called to become the diligent gardener fit to tend Eden's garden.

Therefore he must commune daily through meditation and prayers with the Heavenly Father whom he must live to please. He must care little for the praise of men but look to serve God and humanity sincerely in humility of spirit so that his offerings of love may be well received above. If he is faithful in doing so, the Holy Ghost will inform him about the right seeds to plant and the Holy Spirit will enable him to tend the plants. He will be given to walk along calmly in the knowledge that God will be with him in life always.

There is a certain harmony and orderliness that surrounds life when mankind's footsteps are divinely guided to walk on the righteous path. Such a guided life will be fully settled in Christ to dwell in spiritual fellowship with other members of the divine household. Such a guided one does not walk alone but walks in the company of countless messengers for he has joined the fellowship of the justified that gather around the mercy seat of God. The latter are such that are able to eat of the fig of the tree of life. The fruit of the fig tree is not like that other kind which looks good to the eye but turns out to be bad for man's spirit. The matriarch Eve chose with her eyes instead of her faith and unleashed darkness on mankind. The fig tree bears the fruit of wisdom in accordance with man's obedience and faithfulness in the heavenly way. It is for the pure of heart. The fig tree bears that which the noble in spirit wish from it in faith. It is a wishing tree that accommodates the seed-thoughts of those who have passed judgment before God. Many will try but only a chosen few will find the real tree for there is much wickedness hidden in men's hearts. He that seeks after the fruit of the fig tree must seek after the witness of God and not that of men. The spiritually blind judge by appearance but the pure of heart 'see' and know by faith. Mankind is easily fooled and the enemy does fool many but God cannot be fooled. The nuggets of wisdom are divine seeds entrusted to the faithful. Such are of precious value to humanity and serve to validate those chosen by God. Each one chosen in this light is a channel for divine wisdom and a spiritual giant who walks among men but communes with God in spirit. Such is perceived by those who have embraced Truth and value the real.

Truth washes the heart and imparts nobility to the spirit of man. The noble in spirit can see and know all things as due. If he knocks, the door is opened for him. If he seeks, he finds that which he seeks. If he asks, that which he asks for is given to him. Such that is noble in spirit is given to carry the passport of life for his soul has been reborn for eternal habitation with the Divine. He has become a son of God who together with the other sons traverses the heavenly stairway in twinkling light to bring knowledge from the starry realm down to earth. Such has joined the rank of the immortal beings that can impart life to the withered and dying things on earth. He that traverses the heavenly way in light is a petition bearer to God on behalf of other men. The Heavenly Father interacts with him and he in turn interacts with other men as a divinely appointed mediator. He is like a magnet charged with the essence of

Godliness. He must use that magnetic charge to draw men to God through truth, light and love on to eternal life.

The essence of the Divine is precious and need not be needlessly discharged. Such must be invested to lead blind men back into the light and love of God through Christ. The faithful must keep his flesh on a very short leash for it works to diffuse and discharge the divine essence. The believer that fails to put the essence of godliness to good use is of no use to God or the world for that matter. The salt must not lose its savor for such that does so will be no good for either the land or the dunghill. The faithful one must remain virtuous and firm in spirit so that he can stand on behalf of many that are not able to stand for themselves in the spiritual warfare that bedevils mankind. The chosen have been given access to that which will release many from the imprisonment of darkness and so must stand tall in this regard to be counted worthy.

He who has been charged with the divine essence must not rest on his laurels but must continue to grow in the fullness of the riches of God through Christ. The knowledge, wisdom, judgment and way of God are too deep for man to fully comprehend. The faithful must continue to knock, seek and ask so that he can remain continuously charged in fresh anointing. The power of the Divine is exhaustless and limitless. It can be applied in countless ways to achieve infinite results. It is by continuously reaching towards the Father that the chosen can keep discovering the new within the Divine and grow from glory to glory. Christ Jesus declared that the sons of God who follow after him will do greater things than he has done. In that regard, the chosen that is charged with divine essence has more areas in life to utilize and apply God's power today than his predecessors in days gone by.

The enemy often lulls the unwary into a state of arrested spiritual development. The latter is a kind of spiritual dwarfism where the believer that could have been a giant in God's kingdom falls way short of his potential. He that could have been a Colossian remains a Galatian. He could never defeat the beast of his flesh in 'Ephesus' or move the boulder of material lust out of the way in 'Philippi'. The enemy reasons that if he cannot stop the spread of the kingdom of God that he can at least retard its progress by enticing mankind into sin through the lust of the flesh and earthly material. It is a very effective ploy for the laborer for God is often weary and running on empty. Therefore many professed laborers for God come to compromise their faith walk and settle for much less on account of weariness along the way. The sojourner on the path of righteousness takes a lot of battering from a spiteful world. But it is in the state of weakness that the power of God is made manifest to buttress the faithful. It is also in this state of weakness that the believer will stumble if he does not remain vigilant in spirit.

The key to victory over the beast of the flesh is to remain

covered spiritually and never take off the full armor of God. The key to victory over the boulder of material lust is to continue in sacrificial charity. The faithful believer must never be found spiritually naked nor fail to do what he can for the needy. Hoarding will turn off the faucet of grace and scuttle the vessel of hope. Failure in these areas leads to the idling of the spirit. The idle spirit is the playground of the prince of darkness. The believer will be flooded with the stream of the mundane in his mind when he is idling in spirit. There is never a good time to let one's guard down in the kingdom way for the enemy never quits. To remain victorious in the way, the faithful must keep away from that which he has been forewarned about. The things that he has received forewarning about are those which will spiritually discharge him that aspires for righteousness. The anointing is precious but it must be used for the enlightenment of humanity through Christ. The faithful must obey as God commands for it is by so doing that he will be endued with knowledge to keep him prepared to battle victoriously for God.

✓ Transformative power is availed to remake the believer that partakes worthily of grace.

✓ The faithless that live without light for a long time become slaves to the prince of darkness.

✓ The faithful that puts his trust in God will have his steps directed to live under divine protection.

✓ There is a glow that shows from within the heart that has become an altar lit with the flame of love.

✓ Divine wisdom is dispensed on a need-to-know basis and availed to the believer ready to receive.

✓ The believer bestowed with the key of knowledge must cultivate the rare and precious with patience.

✓ Truth washes and imparts nobility to the faithful to make his spirit able to know in true light.

✓ The power of the Divine is exhaustless and can be applied in infinite ways to do the amazing.

✓ The believer in arrested spiritual development idles in spirit and is soon flooded with the mundane.

Peace comes from not having fear of death

When the old within has made place for a new

Then the enduring and ever-lasting are received

With certainty of faith and in freedom of love

Chapter 24

FROM SEED TO TREE

The aspiring believer can only be transformed into the similitude of Christ if he is willing to pass through the heart of the cross. To pass through the heart of the cross is a Divine calling that only God the Father asks of the chosen. The heart of the cross represents the crossover point between the temporal and the eternal. The believer that willingly endures the attendant suffering to pass through the heart of the cross is given to commute between the exalted realm and the earthly plane. Only the faithful that can soar to the exalted heights in spirit can be of glorious service to God on earth.

The heart of the cross is the point of separation where the world has cast off the believer so to say. By the same token, it is where the believer makes the commitment to double down on God no matter what. The heart of the cross is where the faithful is abandoned by friends, family and many on account of his uncompromising love for God. It is a place where the faithful is grossly and unfairly misunderstood, mischaracterized, derided and often mocked. The heart of the cross is the crucible where the crucial choice between immortality and mortality is made. It is the portal through which the faithful enters into the realm of the perfecting of men into the divine image as sons of God on earth.

The faithful that has passed through the heart of the cross has joined the congregation of the mighty in spirit that stand before God. Such are the sons that walk in greater divine light to oppose spiritual wickedness and afford justice on earth in God's name. At the heart of the cross and beyond is where the spirit has overcome the flesh. It is where the offending portion of the old self is entombed and from where the matured in Christ steps forth to serve God faithfully. It is at that point that the spirit becomes ascendant to lead the flesh always.

The faithful one who passes through the heart of the cross becomes a son of the covenant adopted into the household of the Heavenly Father. He will no longer belong in one place but will belong everywhere. He will no longer belong with anyone but will belong with all men. Such is one who belongs to all yet belongs to none. He will love all men but love God above all else. Such is divinely appointed to walk on earth without fear as God's proxy borne through love. The child of love thinks, speaks and acts in kind. He that has been borne through divine love has come into the place of regeneration where the old things can be made new again for love breeds life.

The journey to the place of regeneration is a long and wearying one that takes a great toll on the faithful. But it is a journey that leads to transformation in spirit, full maturity in Christ and eternity. He that seeks after it must be prepared to lose everything in the world in the interim before he can find that priceless gift in the end. He that finds it will gain everything back in the regeneration that follows in addition to eternal life with the Heavenly Father. It is a long and gradual process in which the tiny seed of faith planted in the believer's garden of the heart grows into full maturity as a tree of righteousness. Through this process the believer is washed in mind, transformed in spirit and fitted in body to serve God gloriously.

Regeneration is life triumphant that snatches victory from the jaws of death. He that has come into regeneration wills and acts under the divine impulse. The regenerated spirit sits at meat with Christ Jesus and the other sons of God under divine love. Such are availed knowledge and wisdom that affords mankind insight into the veiled. Victory in daily living comes about through insightful knowledge. Insightful knowledge is obtained through the Holy Ghost. It is knowledge that avails the words that make it possible to speak to the mountain that stands along life's path to move it out of the way. Problems appear in life but answers to them are found when God is near to empower the seeker with pertinent knowledge.

The faithful that has passed through the heart of the cross into regeneration will always have God near to help. He that is in the place where God is at hand is intimated with the information that he needs to achieve breakthroughs and attain victory in life.

Regeneration is the preserve of those who have passed through the heart of the cross and is the best reserved for last. The power that enables regeneration in the life of the believer comes only from the Heavenly Father who is the giver of life. It is power released exclusively in mercy from the Father to the chosen. He that has come into regeneration is able to receive directly from the throne of the Heavenly Father. He is a son who receives from the Father in mercy and is called to share with others in grace.

Regeneration opens up infinite possibilities and brings about amazing outcomes to the faithful. But much depends on the ability of each son to have his mind focused on the lofty and high things that are pleasing to God. The things that the heart dwells on are the things that mankind aspires to receive in life. The soul that is in regeneration is connected in spirit with the Divine Father and therefore able to bring about whatever the mind conceives through Christ. But he is also one who has been anointed in spirit to teach other men about the divine way. He must therefore remain a light that shines in the midst of darkness for that is his true calling above all else.

The faithful that has come into regeneration is a standard

of reference by which God measures his fellows. He will be constantly provoked in the world but such must learn to be forgiving and merciful always. Much has been divinely ordained for him to do with his time on earth for in regeneration either thoughts, words or actions can cause much to come about. Such is one who no longer gropes about blindly but is guided directly to the heart of every matter. He lives as a witness to men as one committed to truth, simplicity and orderliness in the service of God. He has no problems with telling Truth for it is often in trying to be everything to everyone that the infirm believer compromises faith. It is in trying to be liked by one and all that many seekers are never able to meet up with Christ.

It is in trying to win the praise of men that many believers drift away from the simple and orderly life into the complicated and entangling. The tangled web of life is the domain of the enemy of light who is the prince of the darkness of this world. The misguided, though well-meaning in intention, often falls into the trap of people pleasing to his painful regret. The tendency to please people above all is a slippery slope that often leads the unwary to make compromises and end up in unintended places. There is always a steep and costly price paid in compromising Truth either by trying to appease or keep up appearances with men. To deny or compromise Truth obscures light to invite darkness into mankind's heart. Truth is what defines God and is the foundation for the divine law. He that lives by Truth will have God ever near.

The believer that embraces Truth to live by it soon becomes a dwelling place of the Divine. Out of that heart will spring forth words that are filled with the power of God. Such a heart will become a wellspring of Truth and the transmitter of divine thoughts to mankind. Therefore such a heart that is purified in Truth must focus on uplifting thoughts for his mission in life is to model the way home to the Heavenly Father for others. He will duly become an earthly transmitting station that broadcasts Truth from above to all who hunger for righteousness and the true bread of life. He will come to know on earth as he is known in Heaven by God. In the same wise, he will come to know from Heaven as he is known on earth by men.

As the believer labors to share the message of Christ faithfully, the light of Truth will shine even brighter on, around and for him. His understanding of the veiled truths will deepen. The door of understanding will open widely for him so that his 'glimpse' of the Heavenly Father will become grander and fuller. The Truth that such is given to speak out become appropriate for every matter at hand as one fitly endued with divine wisdom. His words are far from frivolous but Truth directed at the heart of issues. Such are words that break the stony heart so that the goodness therein can be extracted to serve God. Such are also words that induce men of hard exteriors to yield so that they can be shaped into vessels of honor for God. The words of such a faithful heart purified in Truth make things happen for they contain seeds of the spirit of life that inject life into every situation addressed. Such a fountain of the words of life lives to ask, expect, and receive with thanks from God as well as to share with others in love. He is one well prepared to impregnate men's minds with the seeds of such good works that please the Heavenly Father. It is for this reason that he is called not to allow the seeds of his holy vessel to lie fallow but to spread them as needed and thereby plant a heavenly garden on earth.

He that is thusly engaged in cultivating the 'earthly garden that pleases God' is a favorite target of the enemy of light. The latter is always working against God's faithful ones to becloud the mind with earthly cares and worries. Cares and worries breed fear and doubt. Fear and doubt take the lens of the mind out of focus so that a spiritual shadow is cast over the life of the believer. Granted that God's faithful ones may seem to be in the midst of life's storms more often than not yet they pass through them into new and better places every time. When the believer is firmly anchored in faith by trusting God always, peace prevails within the heart even in the midst of life's storms so that he is protected and none the worse for wear.

The faithful one that has embraced Truth to live by it has divine immunity and is shielded from such troubles that will overcome others. He will be able to withstand the battering of life to carry on the good works by which the power of God is glorified among humanity. The most important work is the rescue of the souls lost in seemingly forgotten places that God deems worthy of redemption. The world may forget the erstwhile stranded and seemingly lost soul. But the Heavenly Father who never forgets makes provision for such who will yet prove to be worthy in due time through Christ.

Light catalyzes life but darkness retards it. In order for new life to emerge and flourish, light has to chase darkness away first. The message of Truth through Christ is the light that chases darkness away. The exalted into new life are separated from the world by Truth and the light of Christ. The separation can be likened to a membrane that has tiny holes that are smaller than the proverbial eye of a needle. In order to pass through the 'hole' to be exalted and commune in spirit with God, the faithful must become lowly in spirit through sincerity and humility. Communion with God is the heavenly side of earthly living. It is the small plot of land that costs dearly but wherein that very rare 'precious pearl of life' is hidden. The wise seeker is called to sell all he has if need be in order to afford that small plot. He that has passed through to the Heavenly side has exchanged the confining box of the earthy for the enduring and ever unfolding blossoms of the Divine.

- ✓ The heart of the cross represents the crossover point between the temporal and the eternal.
- ✓ The heart of the cross is where the old is entombed so the new can step forth for glorious service.
- ✓ Spiritual transformation is realized when the tiny seed of faith grows into a tree of righteousness.
- ✓ The faithful that passes through the heart of the cross into regeneration will always have God near.
- ✓ The power of regeneration comes from God and is released in mercy from the Father to sons.
- ✓ The work done in regeneration is carried out through the spirit of God at all hours day and night.
- ✓ The purified heart is a depository from where words that are filled with spirit and power flow.
- ✓ The enemy uses fear and doubt to take the mind out of focus so as to mislead the infirm in spirit.
- ✓ The faithful sanctified in Truth has divine immunity from the things that will destroy other men.
- ✓ The light that the sons bring chases away darkness to catalyze the emergence and flourish of new life.
- ✓ Wisdom is to exchange the confining box of the earthly for the limitless blossoms of the heavenly.

The flame of wisdom is a rare gift that only glows

In minds rid of doubt and fear that love the Truth

With feet guided to take timely and orderly steps

Within hearts open to receive with due thanks

Chapter 25

UNDER DIVINE ILLUMINATION

The wiles and craftiness of the prince of the darkness of this world never ceases. Therefore the son of covenant must always seek greater understanding and knowledge in order to remain steps ahead. The people of God perish not for lack of good effort but mostly for lack of knowledge. Therefore the faithful believer must continuously seek to learn in the better light that comes from living obediently to God's laws. He must aspire for the knowledge and wisdom that is divinely imparted. He that abounds in such knowledge and wisdom will be protected from the evil intentions of the enemy. When greater understanding is followed with faithful living, a brighter divine illumination comes about in the life of the believer. He that is under that greater illumination will twinkle as a star of hope by which his fellows on earth may find their way. Such will ever twinkle as a star as long as he remains a source of enlightenment for other believers to follow after Christ. He will always draw from the well of divine wisdom and receive the wherewithal needed to help him be fruitful in all endeavors.

There are many believers who fall short and are not able to come into the place of greater light or divine illumination. They short-change themselves and fail to receive that which was theirs to possess. Such are the ones who got to the vestibule and walked away never to cross the threshold into the place appointed for them. They failed to step in by not searching out and meditating on the words of Truth. The faithful believer must have strong faith for only such are given strong vision. The seeker after Divine enlightenment has to enter alone into the place of light while there is room. He must not have fear for though he appears to be alone in his journey he is never alone but in the company of 'unseen' spiritual helpers.

As the faithful ponders on a matter of Truth, illumination comes into his mind in momentary flashes of divine inspiration. Veiled knowledge is progressively received from the Divine mind in trickle bits of information but the moment of full understanding is like the flash of lightening in its spontaneity. It is subtle and not as dramatic though. It only connects with the spirit that is ready and the mind that is prepared to receive. The flash of lightning illuminates the dark briefly but it is enough to reveal that which is concealed within. The brief revelation availed by lightning aids the seeker to maintain or change course as necessary. But it will not aid the guilty of heart for such are petrified by the thunder clap that soon follows suit.

The free in spirit is divinely appointed to harness the power of lightning to shred the wall of ignorance that encircles mankind. Lightning transports the ready mind from the present to make the future known. To harness the illumination of lightning is to ride the stream of light. The faithful believer given to ride the stream of light will master time and conquer space. He can travel to wherever needed to answer the Divine call and keep love's appointments. The latter is the mission of healing and restoration through Christ. Divine wisdom is obtained in glimpses in spoonful of love. It is timely distilled from the previously known and reveals itself in ghostlike streaks. It appears from beyond the wall which encircles human consciousness into the present. It is the transfusion of the divine ethos into the moribund in order to bring resuscitation and hope into it. It is the kiss of love that awakens the sleeper when God's day finally dawns for the believer. It is the comforting essence of the Holy Ghost.

The believer that is matured in Christ lives as the free in spirit under the mercy of God. The life fully lived in Christ is one where God's anointing flows freely from Heaven above to the believer below. The anointing works to lift up the less from his lowly state into a higher plane of spiritual enlightenment. It shines needed light so that the relatively blind can begin to see and walk in fellowship with God. It takes a heart willing to commit totally and sacrifice fully in love to help unbelievers embrace Truth. It takes the sort of love that will not let the redeemable go to waste. It is mentally and physically exhaustive work to help the unbeliever find the path of light through Christ. To break the stony heart or to soften the hardened mind is a noble endeavor but very hard to accomplish. It should never be for personal gain but should always be about one brother looking out for another's welfare. It is only when such is the case that the Spirit of God lends aid to make the work become fruitful.

It is only through selfless sacrifice and exemplary charity that faith abounds for the kingdom of God to be established. It is by selflessness and charitable living that the faithful grow into full spiritual maturity in Christ to become God's sons. The faithful have to be 'baptized' in the spirit of Christ in order to be like 'Christ'. Selfless sacrifice carried out in true charity is the baptismal font of Christ. To become Christ one must live like him. The mold has to be the same and the spiritual profile has to fit in the light of Truth and love. In the materially driven world of today, it has become increasingly difficult to live in selfless sacrifice. To be like Christ is a spiritual state that each seeker can realize if God has ordained such for him. It is only God that makes the seemingly impossible for many to become possible for some. The perfecting of the spirit sought after by many is availed by following in the footsteps and living in the way of Christ. It is the only way to be baptized in true light for it cannot be purchased or obtained otherwise. The faithful that has been 'baptized' in the spirit of Christ has met up with the Divine. His old self no longer exists for it has in effect been replaced with the essence of Christ. The new man within the believer that has met up with Christ is one matured in spirit and fitted for adoption as God's son. But he that aspires for such must first overcome the temptations of fame and fortune for that is the mountain in the way for many.

The aspiring seeker has to die in the old self through Christ so that a new can come to full life within him. He must be willing to live selflessly as well as sacrifice fame and fortune as necessary in order for that to come about. He that dies with Christ is given to rise with him also. Therefore the risen in Christ can give life to the dead in spirit. He can resuscitate the dead in sin to new life through Christ for the words of life spring forth from within him. Such is one who can sustain the living and restore the dying through his anointed words. He is able to reap life because he sows life. Life returns to him that passes it along to others. The universe makes room and affords a seat at the table everywhere for the sower of life for he lives as one with the Divine.

He that has died and risen with Christ seeks to have others hearts washed and purified in Truth so that they too can rise in the newness of Christ. This is his calling and nothing is of equal importance to him in life. Such is indeed a man of God but he may not look the part. He is not one the kind that looks saintly on the outside but is ugly within in the spirit as many who loudly profess to follow Christ turn out to be. Nevertheless, the risen in Christ is the saintly in spirit whose heart has been chosen by God as a dwelling place. When God dwells within the heart, the believer is led to devote his life to help the blind see, the lame walk and the dead in spirit live again through Christ. Spiritual blindness leads to a lack of defined purpose in life. Lameness leads to the inability to follow through and accomplish defined objectives. Whereas the dead in spirit can never experience the Divine for he lacks the means within to do so. He that has risen with Christ can help aspiring seekers find the missing that robs them of wholeness in life.

There is a season when the rains cease. This is when the window of grace is closed. This is the season of spiritual accountability when the Heavenly Father looks for figs from the tree that has blossomed with leaves. It is the season when God looks for evidence of Christ from those who profess to follow after him and have partaken of grace in his name. The evidence that God looks for is the heart that is baptized in Truth and lit with the flame of love for all. The close of grace is the season of reprimand for those who have partaken unworthily of grace. It is the season of reprimand for those who did not join the feast of charity in love but for personal gain. Such ones may have gained in the material but those things will come to be of little profit to them when it counts. Those that are reprimanded are not shakers but fakers of faith who look saintly on the outside but are ravenous wolves within.

The faithful that is free from reprimand is a true branch of the tree of righteousness that is laden with figs. The fig is the ability to understand the symbolic language that veils spiritual Truth. The fig is the key to understanding the mysteries of life and the kingdom of God. The platter of figs is about higher and purer Truth communicated with few words. It is the litmus test that ascertains faithfulness and maturity in the way. The fig is the same as the meat of Truth and requires the teeth of wisdom to chew down. Only those who have lived faithfully in the light of Truth to full spiritual maturity through love can understand the hidden things of the Divine.

He that bears figs can communicate with the Divine and all of God's own for the language is borne of same spirit. The fig is figurative language that is traceable to Heaven but applicable on earth. He that can eat figs can understand parables which constitute the language of calibrating earth with the standards of heaven. It is the language by which the Father communicates with his sons on earth. He who bears and eats figs has the attributes of godliness. Such is one who will be given to frame pictures with words with the effortless brilliance of undeniable Truth. A picture is the purest form of communication in that it speaks clearly without words so that there is no misunderstanding. The faithful eater of figs must share the offerings in love so that his fellows on earth may learn them. He that receives in mercy from the Heavenly Father is called to share with those who embrace Truth in good faith through grace. He that has mastered the way that leads to life must walk back to share with those who are yet to find same.

The faithful that shares life's gifts with others in love will have latter rain for God never withholds his tender mercies from such. The latter rain is the shower of blessing that leads into the refreshing and new. It is the dew of the latter rain given to sustain the fig tree. The essence of the fig is the nectar of the new wine which can only be contained by the new wine bottles. The latter are the faithful vessels molded in spirit after Christ who receive duly from God and share as love urges. Such vessels of mercy are the fulfillment of the Father's promise of love and the justification for wisdom. God makes provision for all the ingredients that the merciful needs so that the cocktail of his life is ideal as he serves humanity in love. Heaven's desire is that the merciful ever abound in joy in a foretaste of divine glory availed through Christ. Such becomes mankind's lot in life when he is in covenant with the Divine as a representation of the passing of the former and beginning of the new.

- ✓ The faithful under divine illumination is a star of Hope to help others find the true way.
- ✓ The faithful appear to walk alone but travel in the company of unseen spiritual helpers.
- ✓ Flashes of divine inspiration come to the faithful when the spirit is ready and the mind prepared.
- ✓ Wisdom is timely distilled from the known and revealed within the frame of the 'unknown'.
- ✓ God readily grants the petitions of the believer who has overcome temptations of fame and fortune.
- ✓ The faithful that sows in mercy reaps same for such returns to him that passes it along to others.
- ✓ The dead in spirit can never have experience of the Divine for he lacks the means to receive the pure.
- ✓ The advent season is when God looks for hearts purified in Truth and lit with the flame of love.
- ✓ Divine wisdom affords the key to understand the symbolic language that veils the everlasting.
- ✓ The essence of the tree of life is divine wisdom for those remade as new wine bottles to receive.
- ✓ Mercy serves the golden rule well as fulfillment for love and justification for wisdom.

Mankind often wonders what life's all about

It's but a dress rehearsal for a real to come

Some through wisdom have found the light

And well on their way to the glorious above

Books for Spiritual Guidance by Kalu Onwuka

Nuggets of Resurrection is an engaging discourse that explores the many gifts available to the spiritually matured in Christ, the path that seekers are called to walk as well as how to overcome challenges along the way.

Pulses of the Divine Heart is an uplifting and enriching study that attests to the abiding nature of God's love and the unfailing goodness of Providence to the faithful man whose spirit is in tune with the divine.

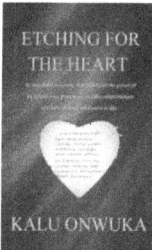

Etching for the Heart is a timely, fascinating and insightful study that highlights the power of sacrificial love, good hope and the enlightenment of Christ to bring wholeness in life of the believer.

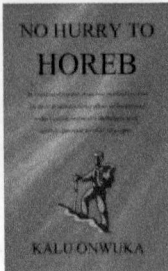

No Hurry to Horeb is a thoughtful discourse about how mankind can tune his inner awareness to rise above the lowliness of today's society and realize the fullness of life divinely appointed for those who truly aspire.

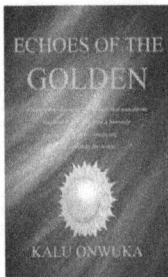

Echoes of the Golden thoughtfully and deeply explores the path that leads to spiritual transformation so that mankind can begin to see from a heavenly perspective to make the earthly experience better.

Books of Original Poems by Kalu Onwuka

Anthems in the Glorious Dawn is a rich collection of ninety-three original poems to nourish the soul, uplift the spirit and help rekindle a relationship with God. The underlying message of the power of sacrificial love strikes a resonant chord.

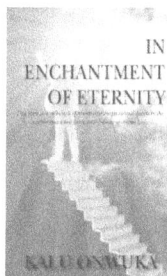

In Enchantment of Eternity is a superb collection of ninety-four original poems that touches the heart deeply through such topics as love, the treasures of life's high road as well as the vision and victory availed through strong faith.

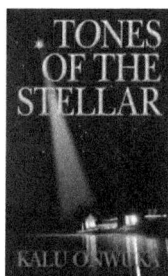

Tones of the Stellar is a volume of eighty eight inspirational poems that speaks to the freedom of spirit and wholeness of life availed by enlightenment through Christ. The remarkable verses offer guidance about reconnecting with God.

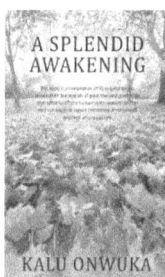

A Splendid Awakening is a simple yet eloquent collection of ninety-two inspirational poems that highlights how man must let go of his mistake-laden past to realize a fulfilling and enduring future full of God's blessing.

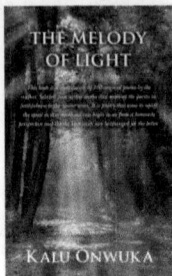

The Melody of Light is a selection from the author's body of work that represents the very best of faith-based poetry. Brimming with insights and thoughtful lessons, the verses paint vivid images about the wholeness that love avails.

All titles are available as paperbacks or e-books and may be purchased through many retail outlets and on-line distribution channels including **amazon.com**. All titles may also be purchased through Granada Publishers at **www.granadapublishing.com** and excerpts of the author's work are available at **www.kaluonwuka.com**.

Kalu Onwuka is a prolific author who writes about faith-walk and the path to transformation within for better in this new age of spiritual awareness. A vanguard among the emerging breed of spiritual poets, he uses his works to highlight the path that mankind must walk in order to find a blissful balance between the earthly and the heavenly.

He is the author of *Ruminations on the Golden Strand* series which are in-depth studies based on spiritual and earthly experiences that frame modern living in a way to help mankind achieve the utmost within a relationship with the Divine. The series include *Nuggets of Resurrection, Pulses of the Divine Heart, Etching for the Faithful Heart, No Hurry to Horeb,* and *Echoes of the Golden.*

He is also the author of *Poems in Faithfulness to the Divine* series which are books of poetry and songs. These include *Anthems in the Glorious Dawn, In Enchantment of Eternity, Tones of the Stellar, A Splendid Awakening* and *The Melody of Light.* There are other works on the way including the forthcoming *Capsules of Divine Splendor.*

Onwuka is a teacher, poet, lyricist, electrical engineer and entrepreneur. He lives in California with his wife of many years with whom he has raised five children. As a follower of Christ Jesus as the Light of the world, he believes that all true spiritual paths eventually converge in Christ. He uses his writing to help many achieve spiritual transformation for a more fulfilling life.